The oversight of souls
Essays on pastoral ministry

This marvelous reminder about the heart of pastoral ministry is must reading for pastors and pastors in training. In our media-driven age, when all too many Christians are enamored with celebrities and all too many churches feature onstage performance more than personal discipleship, Van Neste's bold emphasis on caring for souls is a Godsend. May the Lord use it powerfully to call church leaders back to forming and shepherding the people in our care. And may he use it, as well, to call seminaries back to being schools in which these practices are taught, embodied and commended through in-person, soul-shaping, life-changing pedagogy.

Douglas A. Sweeney
Dean, Beeson Divinity School, Samford University, Birmingham, Alabama

A pastor once shared with me a distressing confession: "I don't love the people of this church." Over many years of working with churches and pastors, it's become clear that loving public speaking, vision casting, programming or building construction is more common than loving "smelly sheep." However, if I understand correctly, these are the very people pastors are commissioned to shepherd. It's all too familiar to hear church members say, "He's a talented speaker, but not much of a pastor."

Dr. Ray Van Neste's insightful book reminds us of the importance of soul care in pastoral roles, with a timely relevance. It's my hope the message in this book will touch us deeply, prompting a reversal of this unfortunate trend. The Chief Shepherd's strategy remains unchanged, yet flocks continue to suffer. Let not the epitaph of your congregation read, "They were as sheep without a shepherd." Gain help in this book.

Jim Elliff
Christian Communicators Worldwide

Ray Van Neste is on to something vital for today's pastor. Having recently, along with Justin Wainscott, edited and republished Theodore Cuyler's great little book, *How To Be a Pastor*, Ray now publishes his own book on the subject, *The Oversight of Souls*. Rooted in faithful exegesis of Scripture and liberally garnished with quotes from Calvin, Bucer, Luther, Baxter and Spurgeon, Dr. Van Neste challenges church shepherds to know their sheep spiritually and deeply through regular personal visitation. It may sound arcane in an age of social media, but nothing could be more relevant or urgent. Van Neste quotes Thomas Chalmers: "A house-going minister makes a church-going people." I commend this book and urge church leaders to read it.

Sandy Willson
Interim president, The Gospel Coalition; pastor emeritus, Second Presbyterian Church, Memphis, Tennessee

I've spent most of my life in pastoral ministry. The challenges of ministry never eased. Despite better skills with study, prayer and experience, the weight of caring for souls lingered. At times I'd grow weary, looking at pastoral work as a job instead of a divinely appointed shepherding ministry for which I would give an account. I needed reminders on such occasions of what it means to be a pastor. For those who know this experience, Ray Van Neste has provided just the resource needed in *The Oversight of Souls*. As a pastor, professor, mentor, pastoral model and doctor of souls, Ray mines Scripture and pastoral history in five biblical, theological and historical essays, setting before pastors the nature and practice of the oversight of souls. Our generation needs the reminders of those who modelled shepherding in far more difficult days, lest we grow soft and anemic in our labours. Pastor, read this book; you'll treasure it. Seminary student, read this book before embarking on pastoral work—and return to it regularly to drink from this spring of pastoral refreshment.

Phil A. Newton
Retired pastor; director of pastoral care & mentoring for the Pillar Network and visiting professor of pastoral theology, Southeastern Baptist Theological Seminary, Wake Forest, North Carolina

The call of a pastor is the oversight of souls. Ray Van Neste has been waving this banner for a long time, which is why I am so thankful to see these essays finally published. This book is beautifully written. Its greatest value is how the author takes the biblical texts that define pastoral ministry and marries them so well with some of the most significant writings on being a pastor from church history. The sources Van Neste uses in his essays alone are worth the price of the book. Every pastor and especially aspiring ones should read this book slowly and carefully.

Brian Croft
Executive director, Practical Shepherding (practicalshepherding.com)

Steeped in the wisdom of the ancients, forged through years of experience and pulsing with scriptural reflection, *The Oversight of Souls* is a succinct yet engaging manual of pastoral theology. Van Neste gives readers a classical vision of soul care that is both timely and timeless. Readers will find themselves compelled to enter this realm of classical shepherding, wondering how they could have believed any other vision of pastoral ministry to be true!

Coleman M. Ford
Assistant professor of humanities, Southwestern Seminary, Fort Worth, Texas, and co-author of *Ancient Wisdom for the Care of Souls*

The oversight of souls

Essays on pastoral ministry

Ray Van Neste

HERITAGE
SEMINARY
PRESS

Heritage Seminary Press, Cambridge, Ontario
An imprint of H&E Publishing, West Lorne, Ontario, Canada
hesedandemet.com

© 2024 Ray Van Neste. All rights reserved. This book may not be reproduced, in whole or in part, without written permission from the publishers.

Cover & book design by Janice Van Eck

The oversight of souls: Essays on pastoral ministry
By Ray Van Neste
ISBN 978-1-77484-154-9 (paperback)
ISBN 978-1-77484-155-6 (eBook)

To my brother, Scott Van Neste,
who has faithfully lived out the pastoral vision I seek
to articulate here, who has borne the brunt of the
pastoral battle, has the scars to show for it, and
even more still has the joy and love of the Master.
Your faithful, joyful perseverance has been a model.
Only eternity will reveal the impact you have had.

Contents

	Preface	xi
	Acknowledgements	xv
1	**The oversight of souls** *Returning to the heart of pastoral ministry*	1
2	**The care of souls** *The heart of the Reformation*	25
3	**Faithful pastoral ministry** *and the "ministry of the Word"*	43
4	**Portrait of a faithful, approved workman** *An exhortation to seminarians (2 Timothy 2:14–26)*	57
5	**Shepherding a rebellious people** *Exodus 32*	75
6	**Brothers, hold fast!**	97

Preface

In 2009 I reworked my course on pastoral ministry at Union University, Jackson, TN, to meet what I saw as a crying need. I included in the syllabus a statement, which I continue to use and which also describes this book:

> It is my conviction that pastoral ministry is at a point of crisis in Western Christianity. As the church has begun taking her cues from the culture, the ideas governing pastoral ministry have become secularized resulting in significant damage to the church. As Lothar of Saxony (twelfth-century Holy Roman emperor) said, "When those who have the title of shepherd play the part of wolves, heresy grows in the garden of the Church." If the church is to be revived and reformed, we must seek a return to biblical priorities in pastoral ministry. This class is intended as a small step toward that grand goal.

As always the path to reform begins with an earnest return to the Scriptures, allowing them to challenge our presuppositions and to set our agenda. Then we must "return to the ancient paths" (Jeremiah 6:16) listening to the church's conversations about interpreting and applying Scripture in reference to pastoral ministry across the ages. Listening only to our own age can serve simply to reinforce our presuppositions. Voices from the past are not correct simply because of their age, but they can challenge our basic assumptions and help us see past the illusion of our era. Thus, we will study together the key biblical texts, wrestling with interpretive issues and concrete applications. We will also read key works on pastoral ministry ranging from the close of the sixth century to the beginning of the twenty-first century. Our cry will be *ad fontes*,[1] and our goal will be to grasp a thoroughly biblical view of pastoral ministry, that we might by God's grace practice biblical pastoral ministry.

In many ways, this book grew out of that pastoral ministry class and my own practical ministry experience. These essays do not address every text or issue relevant to pastoral ministry, but I do seek to speak to the *heart* of pastoral ministry according to the biblical text, read in concert with the church throughout the ages.

Chapter 1 is my argument for a biblical understanding of pastoral ministry. In biblical language—embraced by the church across the ages—pastors are called to the *oversight of souls*. That is why this phrase was chosen for the title of the book. Chapter 2 demonstrates how this understanding of pastoral duty animated and prompted the Reformation and calls us to follow that path. Chapter 3, by examining what is meant in the book of Acts by the phrase, "ministry of the Word," refutes a common misconception of pastoral ministry and a common argument against the necessity of soul care by pastors. Chapter 4 examines Paul's

---

[1] Literally, "to the sources."

exhortation to Timothy in 2 Timothy 2:14–26, seeking to discern the contours of a ministry that is approved by God. Directly addressed to those in training for ministry, it applies just as well to those already engaged in pastoral ministry. One of the key problems with overseeing souls is often those souls do not want overseeing. Chapter 5 treats the golden calf incident (Exodus 32) as an example of shepherding rebellious people, drawing lessons for us today. Then, having argued for a large understanding of the pastoral task, and aware of how daunting it is, the book closes with a word of encouragement, urging pastors to hold fast, trusting the Lord to do *his* work through our faithful though faltering efforts.

It is my earnest prayer that this book will both challenge and encourage pastors, and those considering this high calling. The church is in need of faithful men who will love her and not use her for self-serving grandstanding, for men who will care for souls and not for worldly acclaim, for men who will live for his smile and not care for the approval of men. This is a task worthy of spending and being spent for.

> Every time we look on our congregations, let us believingly remember, that they are the purchase of Christ's blood, and therefore should be regarded by us with the most tender affection.[2]

Ray Van Neste
August 2024

---

[2] Richard Baxter, *The Reformed Pastor* (New York: American Tract Society, 1862), 197–198.

Acknowledgements

Many people have played a part in this book coming together. Groups and individuals are acknowledged in each essay for invitations which gave me the opportunity—and the impetus—to pull my thoughts together. I also appreciate the students who have enrolled in my pastoral ministry class at Union University over the last twenty-plus years where many of these ideas have been hammered out.

Jim Elliff's writings first prodded my thinking in the direction of the oversight of souls. Union University presidents David Dockery and Dub Oliver have encouraged a pastoral vision. David Dockery gave me the invitations, which led to the development of two of these essays. Dub Oliver entrusted me with the role of leading our School of Theology & Missions which led to the opportunity for developing another of these essays.

My colleague and former pastor, Justin Wainscott, has been a particular encouragement in this project as one who shares and has lived out this vision. Mike Garrett, also a colleague and long-time friend, has regularly provided helpful feedback on my essays. Jon Pope, who was in one of my pastoral ministry classes, read the entire manuscript, helping me to shape the essays into a consistent whole. As he has begun his own pastoral ministry, it is a delight to see his faithfulness.

I first began to flesh out these ideas while serving as one of the pastors of Cornerstone Community Church in Jackson, TN, alongside Lee Tankersley and Nathan Young. I owe much to these brothers and that congregation. Tulip Grove Baptist Church in Mt. Juliet, TN, has faithfully prayed for the completion and publication of this book. I am very grateful for their continued interest and care after I had the privilege of serving as their interim pastor. Thank you, Gary LaRoy, for faithfully inquiring each week how you all might pray.

I am grateful to Michael Haykin for his encouragement and thoughts on where to publish this book. I deeply appreciate Janice Van Eck's keen editorial eye as she guided the final stage of the work and often saved me from poor wording.

As always, my wife, Tammie, has been a faithful encouragement, as she has believed in what I do and has nudged me to commit more things to print.

The oversight of souls
Returning to the heart of pastoral ministry[1]

Introduction: Statement of the problem
If pastoral ministry is going to thrive in our churches, we need to regain an understanding of the centrality of the oversight of souls. In fact, I believe the heart of pastoral ministry is this attentive *care of souls*. For many in our day *management* is considered the central aspect of pastoral ministry. For many others *preaching* is considered the most fundamental aspect of pastoral ministry. The renewed emphasis on substantive preaching in many quarters is to be celebrated, but preaching is not the heart of pastoral

---

[1] An earlier form of this chapter appeared as "The Care for Souls: Reconsidering Pastoral Ministry in Southern Baptist and Evangelical Contexts," in *Southern Baptists, Evangelicals, and the Future of Denominationalism*, ed. David S. Dockery (Nashville, TN: B&H, 2011).

ministry; rather preaching is an outflow of oversight. We do not guard souls in order to preach. Rather we preach as one means of guarding souls.

Our central task is not managing good programs, drawing large crowds or even delivering powerful messages. Our central task is shepherding souls as they depart the City of Destruction and hazard their way toward the Celestial City.

It is so easy to forget this or to miss it altogether. And when we do, all else is skewed. Ministry to masses can overshadow the needs of individuals, programs can replace people and sermons can become lightweight pep talks or, even when soundly biblical, they can end up abstract lectures which fail to provide real guidance for people as they struggle with sin, self and Satan.

Put simply, our current setting will, if given half a chance, suck all the personal, pastoral care and concern out of our ministries, replacing it with slick professionalism, which is efficient but impersonal and lacking in real spiritual power.

This lack is being noticed and is showing up in the growing number of books on the discontent of believers with church. Even in 2009, Julia Duin in *Quitting Church*, based on wide and varied interviews, discussed several reasons why otherwise mature believers were deeply disaffected with the church. Among those reasons was the lack of pastoral care. She wrote, "My research suggested that people simply were not being pastored. Often ministers are out of touch with what's happening on the ground."[2]

She cited difficulties people had getting in touch with their pastors or in finding care and guidance for their souls. People often felt they were just supposed to attend mass meetings, fill their cog in the machine and not expect anything more. They did not feel shepherded, or that anyone was engaging their day-to-day world.

In her work Duin interviewed Eugene Peterson who perhaps

---

[2] Julia Duin, *Quitting Church: Why the Faithful Are Fleeing and What To Do About It* (Grand Rapids, MI: Baker, 2009), 22–23.

as much as anyone in our day has thought and written profoundly on the importance of shepherding God's flock, and Peterson said:

> It's the job of pastors, he added, to know about their sheep and not dump the job on a subordinate. "People deserve to have their name known," he said. "They deserve to have somebody who is a spiritual guide and a preacher and pastor to them and who has had a cup of coffee in the kitchen. There is so much alienation, so much loneliness around us. Classically, that is what a pastor does. We've lost that. Of course some people think I'm out to lunch because we don't do that in America. We do something big and influential and cost-efficient. Well, a pastoral life is not cost-efficient, I'll tell you. You don't spend three hours in a nursing home and come away feeling like you've been cost-efficient."[3]

Calvin Miller has written winsomely on this issue in his book *O Shepherd Where Art Thou?* He states,

> Most often when people do leave the church they are leaving because they feel the church failed to minister to them in a time of need. Yet pastors are often more stimulated to make their church grow than to take care of its members in their needy times. No one ever gets his or her picture in an evangelical magazine simply because they visited the sick.[4]

Of course, people are not free to give up on the church just because they are dissatisfied, but we would do well to hear the complaints that are being given to see what substance they have. Duin's research for example traced the lack of connectedness so many people feel, even in places where good sermons are being given. Good preaching is essential. It is just not *all* that is needed.

---

[3] Cited in Duin, *Quitting Church*, 126.
[4] Calvin Miller, *O Shepherd, Where Art Thou?* (Nashville, TN: B&H, 2006), 42.

Larry Crabb has provocatively written:

> Perhaps it is time to screw up our courage and attack the sacred cow: we must admit that simply knowing the contents of the Bible is not a sure route to spiritual growth. There is an awful assumption in evangelical circles that if we can just get the Word of God into people's heads, then the Spirit of God will apply it to their hearts. That assumption is awful, not because the Spirit never does what the assumption supposes, but because it has excused pastors and leaders from the responsibility to tangle with people's lives. Many remain safely hidden behind pulpits, hopelessly out of touch with the struggles of their congregations, proclaiming the Scriptures with a pompous accuracy that touches no one.[5]

Now that is a tough statement. It may be overstated, but there is truth here. It is too easy to remain aloof from our people, failing to get our hands dirty in the day-to-day business of actually applying the truths we preach. This reality has been understood and addressed through the history of the church, and we need to consider this once again.

If we are in earnest about the salvation of souls, we must labour in the teaching of the Word *and* in the careful oversight of the souls of our flock. These two activities cannot rightly be divorced. John Angell James (1785–1859) in his classic book on pastoral ministry, *An Earnest Ministry*, stated, "Good preaching and good shepherding are quite compatible with each other, and he who is in earnest will combine both."[6]

Careful oversight may not make us famous since people cannot download our oversight onto their smartphones, but our preaching cannot be what it ought to be without this care for individual souls.

---

[5] Larry Crabb, *Inside Out* (Colorado Springs, CO: Navpress, 1988), 160.
[6] John Angell James, *An Earnest Ministry: The Want of the Times* (1847; repr. Carlisle, PA: Banner of Truth, 1993), 149.

We need to look again at the Scriptures and the witness of the church through the ages to discern what the heart of pastoral ministry should be. We need to consider the past in order to give perspective to our contemporary conversations. If we only listen to ourselves and our contemporaries, we can fool ourselves into thinking a certain idea is the only way to think, when in fact we may be the first people in history to think this way. By thinking along with the best minds of previous generations we can be, as C.S. Lewis (1898–1963) put it, rescued from "the great cataract of nonsense that pours from the press and the microphone" of our own age.[7]

If you look through the history of the church, you find that the importance of the oversight of souls is not limited to any one denomination, or even to evangelicalism. It is truly part of the Great Tradition. This is an issue where Christians can and should unite.

I cannot here cover all the relevant scriptural texts or historical affirmations. I will focus on some key texts and then in the discussion of these texts use selected quotes from across the range (chronologically and ecclesiastically) of church history. The historical witness alongside scriptural texts serves to demonstrate that this reading of Scripture is not unique but is the common voice of the church.[8]

Scriptural texts on pastoral ministry

We are not at a loss for texts about pastoral ministry though it seems they are not referenced enough. When thinking of the pastor's role we ought to look first to Jesus himself, the "Great Shepherd of the sheep" (Hebrews 13:20). In John 10, Jesus describes himself as the true Shepherd and in so doing gives us a picture of what true under-shepherds should be as well:

---

[7] C.S. Lewis, "Learning in War-Time," in *The Weight of Glory: And Other Addresses* (San Francisco, CA: Harper Collins, 1980), 58–59.

[8] Chapter two examines more fully the witness of the Reformation era to this point.

> I am the good shepherd. The good shepherd lays down his life for the sheep. He who is a hired hand and not a shepherd, who does not own the sheep, sees the wolf coming and leaves the sheep and flees, and the wolf snatches them and scatters them. He flees because he is a hired hand and cares nothing for the sheep. I am the good shepherd. I know my own and my own know me, just as the Father knows me and I know the Father; and I lay down my life for the sheep (John 10:11–15).

Undoubtedly one reason the term "pastor" or "shepherd" is used in the New Testament of pastors is to connect with the work and example of Jesus as the Great Shepherd. Notice, first of all, the care given to the sheep. The true under-shepherd must be one who does not run at the approach of danger. Rather he is one who stands by his post defending the sheep even giving his life if necessary. In the fourth century, John Chrysostom (d. AD 407) applied this passage to pastoral ministry stating,

> A great thing, beloved, a great thing is the role of leader in the Church. It is one that requires much wisdom, and as great courage as Christ's words indicate: namely, sufficient to lay down one's life for the sheep; sufficient never to leave them unprotected and exposed to danger; and sufficient to stand firm against the attack of the wolf.[9]

Notice also that Jesus explicitly says he knows his sheep. There is no way to guard the sheep if you do not know them.

Alexander Maclaren commenting on this passage wrote:

---

[9] John Chrysostom, "Homily 60," in *Saint John Chrysostom: Commentary on Saint John the Apostle and Evangelist (Homilies 48–88)*, vol. 41 of *The Fathers of the Church: A New Translation*, ed. Roy Joseph Deferrari (New York: Fathers of the Church, 1959), 133.

Individualising care and tender knowledge of each are marks of the true shepherd. To call by name implies this and more. To a stranger all sheep are alike; the shepherd knows them apart. It is a beautiful picture of loving intimacy, lowliness, care, and confidence, and one which every teacher should ponder. Contrast this with the Pharisees' treatment of the blind man.[10]

More on this later.[11]

Next, we look at perhaps the key text in this discussion, Hebrews 13:17:

> Obey your leaders and submit to them, for they are keeping watch over your souls, as those who will have to give an account. Let them do this with joy and not with groaning, for that would be of no advantage to you.

Notice that this passage posits significant authority in the pastors (and it is not really softened by translating "obey" as "be persuaded by"). Notice also though, this authority is directly tied to the work of watching over souls. Pastors have authority in the church precisely because they are to be guarding souls. And, then, the Scripture makes the important point that pastors are to engage the work of this oversight in a manner shaped by the realization that God himself will call them to account. Here we

---

[10] Alexander Maclaren, *The Gospel of St. John*, Bible Class Expositions (London: Hodder and Stoughton, 1893), 106.

[11] After studying this passage in John in my pastoral ministry class, one student wrote:

> This passage is an encouragement to me as one who feels called to preach the Word of God. If I become a pastor, I must love the sheep like Jesus did. I must be willing to die for my flock and guard my flock from wolves. I must be willing to encourage and rebuke my flock and always do what is for their eternal good. I must set an example for them in everything so that their faith may not be shaken by my poor leadership. What an enormous responsibility awaits me. May I never take it lightly.

are given a clear statement about what God expects of pastors and what he will hold us accountable for on the final day. No mention is made here of drawing crowds, building buildings or managing programs. Those things may be fine, but in the end what matters is the oversight of souls.

But what is meant here by "watch over souls"? The term is used elsewhere with the sense of watchfulness, staying awake, guarding and protecting. We are to keep watch over our congregations, protecting them and guiding them by providing clear biblical teaching and personally rebuking and encouraging. As John Owen (1616–1683) in the seventeenth century wrote:

> And the apostle compriseth herein the whole duty of the pastoral office.... The work and design of these rulers [pastors] is solely to take care of your souls,—by all means to preserve them from evil, sin, backsliding; to instruct them and feed them; to promote their faith and obedience; that they may be led safely to eternal rest. For this end is their office appointed and herein do they labour continually.[12]

This idea is why Martin Bucer (1491–1551), leader of the Reformation in Strasbourg in the sixteenth century, titled his treatise on pastoral ministry, *Concerning the True Care of Souls*. It is striking also that he refers to a pastor as *Seelsorger*, a "carer of souls."[13]

This will require personal knowledge of the sheep. It will not be accomplished merely by sermons fired at random. We again must be like the Good Shepherd who pursues the wandering sheep. This task cannot be fulfilled in the pulpit alone. It requires us to commit to following up with our people. As a pastor I taught our people that we say to fellow members, "We will love you

---

[12] John Owen, *The Works of John Owen*, ed. William H. Goold (London: Johnstone and Hunter, 1855), 465.

[13] Martin Bucer, *Concerning the True Care of Souls*, trans. Peter Beale (Carlisle, PA: Banner of Truth, 2009), vii.

enough to chase you down should you ever wander away. You can choose to break your connection with us but you will not just slip away and be forgotten."

John Erskine (1721–1803) an eighteenth century Scottish Presbyterian wrote:

> Sermons, like arrows shot at a venture, seldom hit the mark when we do not know the character of our hearers; and, in many instances, our knowledge of their character must be imperfect if we contract no familiarity with them.[14]

Similarly, Charles Brown (1806–1884), in Scotland in the ninteenth century also wrote:

> After a long ministry I do not hesitate to express my belief, that…the best preaching will lose much of its power without the systematic visiting of the flock at their homes.
>
> Not only must the minister remain thus a stranger, to a large extent, to their condition and necessities, and so have to preach to them very much at random, but he shall fail of securing that kindly esteem and affectionate confidence at their hands, without which, however he may win their mere respect by his pulpit ministrations, his preaching will probably fail to a great extent of its grand use and end. As the people will most surely bid that minister right welcome to their homes whose voice they hear with joy on the Sabbaths, so will they return with fresh and ever-growing joy to the church, to listen to *his* voice whom they have found the sympathizing friend and counselor of their loved families.[15]

---

[14] John Erskine, "Difficulties of the Pastoral Office," in *The Christian Pastor's Manual*, ed. John Brown (1826, 1991; repr., Morgan, PA: Soli Deo Gloria, 2003), 191–192. Erskine goes on to comment on how difficult this is with a large congregation.

[15] Charles J. Brown, *The Ministry: Addresses to Students of Divinity* (Carlisle, PA: Banner of Truth, 2006), 84.

A similar point was made by ninteenth-century New England Congregationalist Silas Aiken (1799–1869):

> A particular oversight and care of the flock…is involved in the idea of the pastoral work…and can no more be pushed aside or ignored, than any other part. …the man who assumes the sacred office, and, in the neglect of the personal inspection and private instruction of the souls committed to his care, thinks to discharge his obligations by his pulpit labors, is sadly derelict in duty. He sets aside the scriptural model, and sets up a standard of his own devising instead.[16]

This is what is in view when in the New Testament pastors are called *overseers*. This does not refer to management in our business model, but to the task of overseeing *souls*, watching out for the flock, fighting off wolves and pursuing wandering sheep.

This theme is also found in Peter's famous exhortation to pastors in 1 Peter 5:

> So I exhort the elders among you, as a fellow elder and a witness of the sufferings of Christ, as well as a partaker in the glory that is going to be revealed: shepherd the flock of God that is among you, exercising oversight, not under compulsion, but willingly, as God would have you; not for shameful gain, but eagerly; not domineering over those in your charge, but being examples to the flock. And when the Chief Shepherd appears, you will receive the unfading crown of glory (1 Peter 5:1–4).

Here we are told to *shepherd* and *exercise oversight*. These two activities cannot be fully covered by preaching. Certainly preaching is an important element, but shepherding in these contexts

---

[16] Silas Aiken, "On Pastoral Duties," *The Congregational Quarterly* 8 (January 1866): 30.

would also conjure up the image of guarding, pursuing and personal care.

These themes also show up in Paul's farewell address to the Ephesian elders in Acts 20:

> You yourselves know how I lived among you the whole time from the first day that I set foot in Asia, serving the Lord with all humility and with tears and with trials that happened to me through the plots of the Jews; how I did not shrink from declaring to you anything that was profitable, and teaching you *in public and from house to house*, testifying both to Jews and to Greeks of repentance toward God and of faith in our Lord Jesus Christ.... *Pay careful attention to yourselves and to all the flock, in which the Holy Spirit has made you overseers, to care for the church of God, which he obtained with his own blood* (Acts 20:18–21, 28, italics added).

This passage is significant as Paul's summary of his own ministry. At this point, some readers might find themselves thinking, "But the apostles in Acts 6 said their priority was to be the ministry of the Word and prayer. How does this fit with what you are saying?" This passage shows how it fits very well. Paul shows his ministry of the Word involved not only public proclamation but also proclamation "from house to house." If we would follow the apostolic pattern, we must give public *and* private instruction.[17] As we spend time with the people in our congregation, we speak truth to them in the midst of everyday life, as well as preaching it on Sunday. This every-day, private ministry is so important, showing that what is discussed in church is really supposed to be lived out in daily life.

This is also affirmed in the Westminster *Directory of Public Worship* (1645) which says,

---

[17] This topic is pursued further in chapter 3.

> It is the duty of the minister not only to teach the people committed to his charge in public, but privately; and particularly to admonish, exhort, reprove, and comfort them, upon all seasonable occasions, so far as his time, strength, and personal safety will permit.[18]

As Richard Baxter (1615–1691) cautioned, "I fear most those ministers who preach well, and who are unsuited to the private nurture of their members."[19] Rather, this sort of pastoral ministry grows out of real care and affection for the people under our care. This is simply not a task that can be done with our hearts carefully tucked away.

I have often heard young pastors counselled not to get too close to their church members. They are encouraged to keep a "professional" or even "prophetic" distance. In one case the advice was that getting too close would make it too difficult to deliver rebuke when needed. This advice is not only unhelpful, it is downright ungodly! Rebuke ought not be delivered if it is too easy. It is the wounds of a friend that are faithful,[20] not the cool correction of a hired hand.

Such emotional distance is not the biblical model. Notice what Paul writes to the Thessalonians:

> For you yourselves know, brothers, that our coming to you was not in vain.... But we were *gentle among you, like a nursing mother taking care of her own children.* So, *being affectionately desirous of you, we were ready to share with you not only the gospel of God but also our own selves, because you had become very dear to us.*

---

[18] "Concerning Visitation of the Sick," in *The Directory for the Public Worship of God, Agreed Upon by the Assembly of Divines at Westminster 1645* (1845; repr., New York: Robert Kennedy, 1880), 32.

[19] Richard Baxter, *The Reformed Pastor* (1656), rev. ed., ed. James M. Houston (Portland, OR: Multnomah, 1982), 7.

[20] Proverbs 27:6.

For you remember, brothers, our labor and toil: we worked night and day, that we might not be a burden to any of you, while we proclaimed to you the gospel of God. You are witnesses, and God also, how holy and righteous and blameless was our conduct toward you believers. For you know how, *like a father with his children, we exhorted each one of you and encouraged you* and charged you to walk in a manner worthy of God, who calls you into his own kingdom and glory.

For what is our hope or joy or crown of boasting before our Lord Jesus at his coming? Is it not you? For you are our glory and joy (1 Thessalonians 2:1, 7–12, 19–20, italics added).

Does this sound like a man who has been careful not to get his affections wrapped up with his people? Of course not! The only way we will "labor and toil" working "night and day" is if our people become "very dear to us" so that we are "affectionately desirous" of them. And this sort of affection will only grow as you get to know them, walk with them, share in their joys and sorrows and then permit them to walk alongside you sharing your joys and griefs as well. Then we will treat them like gentle mothers and concerned fathers.

The great Reformer, Martin Luther (1483–1546), is often known for being fiery and even rough. Yet notice how he speaks of the love of a pastor for his congregation:

> Men who hold the office of the ministry should have the heart of a mother toward the church; for if they have no such heart, they soon become lazy and disgusted, and suffering, in particular, will find them unwilling.... Unless your heart toward the sheep is like that of a mother toward her children- a mother, who walks through fire to save her children—you will not be fit to be a preacher. Labor, work, unthankfulness, hatred, envy, and all kinds of sufferings will meet you in this

office. If, then, the mother heart, the great love, is not there to drive the preachers, the sheep will be poorly served.[21]

Moving forward one century, to the seventeenth, Samuel Rutherford (1600–1661) is a powerful example of deep affection for one's congregation. Having been torn away from his people and exiled for his devotion to the gospel, Rutherford wrote letters to his people exhorting, counselling, challenging and teaching them. The collection of these letters is now considered a spiritual classic. In one letter in particular, he addressed his congregation as a whole:

> Dearly beloved and longed-for in the Lord, my crown and my joy in the day of Christ, Grace be to you, and peace from God our Father, and from our Lord Jesus Christ.
> I long exceedingly to know if the oft-spoken-of match betwixt you and Christ holdeth, and if ye follow on to know the Lord. My day-thoughts and my night-thoughts are of you; while ye sleep I am afraid of your souls, that they be off the rock. Next to my Lord Jesus and this fallen kirk, ye have the greatest share of my sorrow, and also of my joy; ye are the matter of the tears, care, fear, and daily prayers of an oppressed prisoner of Christ. As I am in bonds for my high and lofty One, my royal and princely Master, my Lord Jesus; so I am in bonds for you.... What could I want, if my ministry among you should make a marriage between the little bride in those bounds and the Bridegroom? Oh, how rich a prisoner were I, if I could obtain of my Lord (before whom I stand for you) the salvation of you all! Oh, what a prey had I gotten, to have you catched in Christ's net! Oh, then I had cast out my Lord's lines and His net with a rich gain! Oh then, well-wared pained breast, and sore back, and crazed

---

[21] Martin Luther, "Ministers" in *What Luther Says: A Practical In-Home Anthology for the Active Christian*, ed. Ewald M. Plass (1959; repr., Saint Louis, MO: Concordia, 1994), 932.

body, in speaking early and late to you!... My witness is above; your heaven would be two heavens to me, and the salvation of you all as two salvations to me. I would subscribe a suspension, and a fristing of my heaven for many hundred years (according to God's good pleasure), if ye were sure in the upper lodging, in our Father's house, before me.[22]

This is a pastor's heart!

When we have this sort of affection for our people, we will be able to say of our churches the sort of things we find the apostle Paul saying, "For now we live, if you are standing fast in the Lord" (1 Thessalonians 3:8). This also then explains Paul's description of his pastoral aims in Colossians:

> Now I rejoice in my sufferings for your sake, and in my flesh I am filling up what is lacking in Christ's afflictions for the sake of his body, that is, the church, of which I became a minister according to the stewardship from God that was given to me for you, to make the word of God fully known, the mystery hidden for ages and generations but now revealed to his saints. To them God chose to make known how great among the Gentiles are the riches of the glory of this mystery, which is Christ in you, the hope of glory. Him we proclaim, *warning everyone and teaching everyone* with all wisdom, that we may present *everyone* mature in Christ. For this I toil, struggling with all his energy that he powerfully works within me (Colossians 1:24–29, italics added).

Part of what is striking in this passage is the emphasis on individuals. Paul sought to warn and teach each member with the goal of presenting *each one* mature in Christ. This aim should animate our ministries. Too often today leaders are content with

---

[22] Samuel Rutherford, "Letter 225", *Letters of Samuel Rutherford*, 5th ed. (Edinburgh, UK: Oliphant Anderson & Ferrier, n.d.), 438–439.

seeing maturity or even attendance in a "significant percentage" of the membership. But this is not Paul's aim. We are to labour and suffer to see that each one attains maturity in Christ. John Calvin (1509–1564) wrote,

> The office of a true and faithful minister is not only publicly to teach the people over whom he is ordained to pastor, but, so far as may be, to admonish, exhort, rebuke, and console each one in particular.[23]

One of the early Baptist confessions of faith includes the following affirmation:

> That the members of every church or congregation ought to know one another, so they may perform all the duties of love to one another, both spiritually and physically. (Matt. 18:15; 1 Thes. 5:14; 1 Cor. 12:25) And especially the elders ought to know the whole flock over which the Holy Spirit has made them overseers. (Acts 20:28; 1 Pet. 5:2-3) Therefore a church ought not to consists of such a multitude that each member cannot have individual knowledge of one another.[24]

Furthermore, Henry Scougal (1650–1678), prominent Scottish pastor and theologian who profoundly influenced both George Whitefield and the Wesley brothers, wrote:

> But certainly the greatest and most difficult work of a minister is in applying himself particularly to the various persons under his charge; to acquaint himself with their behaviour and the temper of their souls; to redress what is amiss and

---

[23] John Calvin, "Visitation of the Sick," in *John Calvin: Tracts and Letters*, vol. 2, ed. by Henry Beveridge (1849; repr., Carlisle, PA: Banner of Truth, 2009), 127.

[24] "A Declaration of Faith of English People Remaining at Amsterdam in Holland" (1611), in *Baptist Confessions of Faith*, rev. ed., ed. William L. Lumpkin (Valley Forge, PA: Judson Press, 1959), 121.

prevent their future miscarriages. Without this private work, his other endeavors will do little good....

Now this supposes a great deal of care, to acquaint ourselves with the humors and conversation of our people; and the name of "watchmen" that is given to us implies no less.[25]

Furthermore, Richard Baxter, considered by some, the consummate pastor, wrote eloquently on this subject in his classic book, *The Reformed Pastor*. Here are some pertinent samples, which really sum up the argument to this point:

> But our second concern must also be for *individuals* in the church. We need therefore to know every person that belongs to our charge. For how can we take heed to them unless we know them? We should know completely those in our flock. As a careful shepherd looks after every individual sheep, or as a good schoolmaster looks after every individual student, or as a good doctor knows each of his patients—in these ways we should know them. Christ Himself, the great and good Shepherd, takes care of every individual.... We, too, must give an account of our watch over the souls of all that are bound to obey us (Hebrews 13:7). Many more passages of Scripture assure us that it is our duty to take heed to every individual person that is in our flock. And many passages in the ancient church council do plainly tell us that it was also the practice in those days to do likewise. In one passage, Ignatius says, "Let assemblies be often gathered; inquire into all by name, despise not servant-men or maidens" So you see it was then taken as a duty to look upon every member of the flock by name, even if it should be the meanest servant-man or maid....

---

[25] "On the Importance and Difficulty of the Ministerial Function," in *The Works of the Rev. Henry Scougal*, ed. Don Kistler (1765; repr. Morgan, PA: Soli Deo Gloria, 2002), 241, 252.

A faithful pastor should have his eyes on them all. He should labor to know each person's natural temperament, their situations, and the context of their affairs in the world. A pastor should be aware of the company they live with and deal with, so that he may know where their temptations lie. Thus he knows speedily, prudently, and diligently how to help them.[26]

In summing up his book, Baxter gives twenty points on the benefits of attending to each individual in the congregation. In this context he makes these statements:

> But when a minister does not know his own people, he is not able to really minister to them. By means of such personal ministry we come to be better acquainted with each one's spiritual state. Then we know better how to watch over them and relate to them….
>
> They should see us not as simply necessary for their emergency situations. They should see themselves as disciples or scholars who are being taught by their pastors through personal advice and given help for their salvation."[27]

Theodore Cuyler (1822–1909), pastor of the largest Presbyterian congregation in the United States in the late nineteenth century, also fully embraced this vision of pastoral ministry. He was concerned enough to inculcate this approach to ministry, that after his retirement he wrote a book, *How To Be a Pastor*, to commend such ministry to young pastors. He urged, "The importance of all that portion of a minister's work that lies *outside of his pulpit* can hardly be overestimated."[28] He went on to say:

---

[26] Baxter, *The Reformed Pastor*, 71–72, 76.

[27] Baxter, *The Reformed Pastor*, 107–108.

[28] Theodore L. Cuyler, *How To Be a Pastor: Wisdom from the Past for Pastors in the Present*, ed. Ray Van Neste and Justin Wainscott (1890; Eugene, OR: Wipf & Stock, 2024), 2.

Of course, if you are a faithful pastor, you will secure a regular visit to every family in your flock once (or oftener), in every year. But extra emergencies demand an extra call promptly. Sudden affliction demands an immediate visit.[29]

Upon his retirement, Cuyler told his people, "It has been my rule to know everybody in this congregation, if possible, and seldom have I allowed a day to pass without a visit to some of your homes."[30]

As a Baptist, let me now include some Baptist voices to show the solidarity of Baptists with this stream of thought.

P.H. Mell (1814–1888) was a delegate at the founding of the Southern Baptist Convention (SBC) in the USA, who went on to serve as president of the SBC for fourteen years. Mell was known as a powerful, doctrinal preacher. His biographer records this account of his ministry:

Very much of his power as a preacher lay in the way he had of getting close to his people. His custom was to visit *all* of them, and so anxious were they not to miss the expected pleasure that he made engagements ahead often as far as three months. The humblest householder was glad to entertain "Brother Mell," and the same ease of manner characterized him whether he sat at the bountiful board of the rich, or broke the plain bread and partook of the cup of milk from the pine table of the poorest.... If a poor man was harassed with debt, broken hearted over a willful child, or bowed down with bereavement, he never felt his load to be quite so heavy after he had talked it over with "Brother Mell."[31]

Moving to the Northeast, Hezekiah Harvey (1821–1893) was a prolific Baptist pastor and professor at Hamilton Theological

---

[29] Cuyler, *How To Be a Pastor*, 9.
[30] Cuyler, *How To Be a Pastor*, 64.
[31] P.H. Mell, Jr., *The Life of Patrick Hues Mell* (Harrisonburg, VA: Gano Books, 1991), 61–62.

Seminary. In his treatise on pastoral ministry, he wrote:

> The care of souls is the radical idea of the pastor's office. He is a shepherd to whom a flock has been committed to guide, to feed, to defend; and the divine command enjoins: "Take heed to *all* the flock, over the which the Holy Ghost hath made you overseers" (Acts 20:28). He is to be the personal religious guide, the confidential Christian friend, of his charge. Our Lord, in his description of the Good Shepherd, said, "The sheep hear his voice; and he calleth his own sheep by name, and leadeth them out. And when he putteth forth his own sheep, he goeth before them, and the sheep follow him; for they know his voice" (John 10:3–4). Each member of his flock is a soul entrusted to his care by the Lord; and if true to his trust, he is one of those who "watch for souls as they who must give account." Paul, when in Ephesus, taught not only publicly, but "from house to house;" and in his farewell charge to the elders of that city he said, "Watch, and remember that, by the space of three years, I ceased not to warn every man night and day with tears" (Acts 20:31).[32]

Then there is Charles Bray Williams (1869–1952) who was founding New Testament professor at Southwestern Baptist Theological Seminary in Fort Worth, Texas, chair of New Testament Interpretation at Mercer University in Macon, Georgia, and professor of Greek and Ethics at Union University in Jackson, Tennessee, where he published his translation of the New Testament. Throughout this work, he was also a pastor. His daughter, Mrs. Charlotte Williams Sprawls has written a biographical sketch of her father where she recollects his pastoral ministry in his later years, in his eighties, when he was pastoring a 700-plus member church. She wrote, "[He] believed strongly

---

[32] Hezekiah Harvey, *The Pastor: His Qualifications and Duties* (Philadelphia, PA: American Baptist Publication Society, 1879), 78.

in a pastor's knowing personally every member in his church, and he had a very active plan of visitation of every family in their home every few weeks."[33] That is quite a testimony for a man at that age and a church of that size.

Lastly, I could point to W.A. Criswell (1909–2002), who in his guidebook for pastors writes:

> The shepherd tending his flock, the pastor living in love and encouragement among his people, is the picture the New Testament presents of this God-called servant.... Prayer, even fervent prayer, is not enough, nor is prayer plus incessant Bible study enough. We must also live with our people, minister to our people, encourage, and guide our people.... If the pastor would really succeed in his work, let him minister to the needs of his people. ...the pastor who knows, loves, visits, and ministers to his flock has a place in their hearts sacred forever....
>
> The example of the great pastors of the world is always one of personal contact with the people. The pulpit is the throne of the preacher, but the throne is not stable unless it rests on the affections of the people. To win the affections of the people, you must visit with them and know them and talk to them and let them talk to you. The man with whom you have wisely and tenderly conversed on vital, personal religion cannot turn a cold, critical ear toward you on the Lord's Day, nor does he. The man who visits has the love of the people.[34]

---

[33] Charlotte Williams Sprawls, *Charles Bray Williams: Greek Scholar, Professor, Writer, Pastor and Preacher, 1896–1952*; Translator of "The New Testament in the Language of the People" (Graceville, FL: Florida Baptist Historical Society, 2007), 12.

[34] W.A. Criswell, *Criswell's Guidebook for Pastors* (Nashville, TN: Broadman Press, 1980), 273–275.

Conclusion

The oversight of souls is the *heart* of pastoral ministry. From this effort of caring for souls comes preaching, visiting, counselling and everything else a pastor does. We preach in order to guard and guide souls. We pray for them that they might hate sin, love God, be encouraged and persevere. We visit and counsel so that we might point them in the way of truth and that they may overcome the snares of sin. And, while there are various reasons why we pursue personal holiness, one reason is the fear of harming our dear people.

Brothers, let us *shepherd* God's sheep. He bought them with his own blood! Is there anything more valuable, more worthy of our attention? His saving of them was not haphazard or random. Neither should our care of them be.

On the final day, we will be called to give an account before God himself, and he will not inquire of our buildings, programs, etc. He has told us he will examine how we cared for the souls of those entrusted to our care. Let us consider this soberly and pursue our ministries accordingly. This will likely have radical implications for what we do and how we do it. Let us pursue this goal relentlessly, since it is the clear command of our Master, the Great Shepherd of the sheep. Let us imitate him so we might please him and know his pleasure upon our lives.

Fellow pastors, we have been entrusted with a group of people who are feeble and frail, who still struggle with sin and get frightened and overwhelmed. Our task is to guide them faithfully on to heaven, fighting off the wolves, warning of snares, even chasing out false sheep.

Horatius Bonar (1808–1889), that wonderful Scottish pastor, ardent evangelist and hymnwriter said it well:

> To this extent the office of the elder and the minister is the same. The design of both is *the oversight of souls*....
>
> Oh! Remember, then, that it is for the care of souls that you have been now ordained; it is for souls that you are to

labour, and watch, and pray; and it is for souls that you are to give an account when the great Shepherd shall appear.[35]

May we be found faithful in this task.

---

[35] Horatius Bonar, "The Union Between Christ and Believers, and the Union of Believers One With Another: A Discourse," *The Scottish Christian Herald* 2 (Jan.–Dec. 1840): 748.

The care of souls
The heart of the Reformation[1]

Introduction

The Reformation is often dismissed as an academic discussion involving debates about the finer points of theology and lofty ideas of interest to some people but disconnected from real-life issues, struggles and heartache. It is important for us to be rescued from such notions lest this important event in our history become yet one more dusty item on the shelf, pulled out for special occasions but otherwise forgotten. As Ronald Wallace writes,

---

[1] An earlier version of this essay was published as "The Care of Souls: The Heart of the Reformation," *Themelios* 39.1 (April 2014): 53–63. This essay originally began as an address for the Reformation Day chapel on October 31, 2012, at Union University in Jackson, Tennessee. I am grateful to Jim Patterson, who helped me chase down some sources for this essay. Before being a colleague at Union, he was my first church history professor. His class on the Magisterial Reformation was a joy and a formative influence, no doubt contributing to this essay beyond what I am aware.

"The Reformation itself was a pastoral care movement growing directly out of care for the salvation of the soul."[2]

The Reformation was a diverse movement, but at its centre was a pulsing, yearning concern for the well-being of souls. Its leaders were pastors at pains to lead their flock—and others from around the world—to forgiveness before God and the resultant living hope, the knowledge of God's care and presence in the real hardships of this world and the certain hope of resurrection.

1. Pastoral care

One of the objects the Reformers most commonly attacked was the overly speculative theology of the medieval Scholastic theologians.[3] Take, for example, the event pointed to as the launching pad of the Reformation: Luther's posting his *Ninety-Five Theses*. What provoked this? Not academic subtleties or political aspiration, but instead a moment of pastoral, "Oh, no you don't!" The issue was that Johann Tetzel arrived telling Luther's people they could buy God's grace and forgiveness without any concern for faith or repentance.[4] Tetzel was toying with the fears of the people and manipulating their emotions: "Are you so tight-fisted not to pay now so that dear grandma can escape the torments of

---

[2] Ronald Wallace, *Calvin, Geneva and the Reformation: A Study of Calvin as Social Reformer, Churchman, Pastor and Theologian* (Grand Rapids: Baker, 1988), 169. So also John T. McNeill, *A History of the Cure of Souls* (New York: Harper & Row, 1951), 163: "In matters concerning the cure of souls the German Reformation had its inception."

[3] "The Reformation was a movement of applied theology and lived Christianity. It was not anti-intellectual, but it was antiabstractionist." See Timothy George, *Reading Scripture with the Reformers* (Downers Grove: IVP, 2011), 228.

[4] The indulgence sale was not authorized in the region where Luther ministered, but was authorized in the neighbouring region. Tetzel plied his trade just across the Elbe River from Wittenberg, and people came from all around to purchase them. Some of Luther's famous *Ninety-Five Theses* explicitly address the sale of indulgences (eg. 27, 28). For more on indulgences, Tetzel, and Luther's opposition, see Bard Thompson, *Humanists and Reformers: A History of the Renaissance and Reformation* (Grand Rapids, MI: Eerdmans, 1996), 394–400; F.L. Cross and E.A. Livingstone, eds., "Tetzel, Johann," in *The Oxford Dictionary of the Christian Church*, 3rd ed. (Oxford: Oxford University Press, 1997), 1605.

purgatory? Are you so hard hearted as to not give your last penny to allow your dear, departed mother to find relief? As soon as a coin in the coffer rings a soul from purgatory springs!"

Luther, in light of his new understanding of justification, recognized this treachery and the damning effects it would have on unsuspecting souls duped by it. His opposition sprang from an earnest desire to shepherd souls and guide them safely to heaven.[5]

As noted in chapter 1, Luther said pastors must

> have the heart of a mother toward the church; for if they have no such heart, they soon become lazy and disgusted, and suffering, in particular, will find them unwilling.... If, then, the mother heart, the great love, is not there to drive the preachers, the sheep will be poorly served.[6]

It is this love for people that drove Luther's ministry. He not only wrote theological treatises, took on the powers of the world of his day and endured death threats, but also counselled hundreds in person and in his letters and attended to countless aspects of daily ministry, including writing a guide for teaching children. Once his barber told him he struggled with prayer, so Luther

---

[5] See the similar comment by George, *Reading Scripture*, 233: "It was his concern for the care of souls in his charge, as much as his scholarly work as a university professor, that propelled Luther to take a public stand on indulgences." Owen Chadwick wrote, "The Indulgence he believed to be pernicious because it was misleading simple souls."See *The Reformation* (London: Penguin, 1972), 46. David Cornick assesses that Luther's "reaction to the indulgence campaign of 1516/17 was that of a pastor." See "The Reformation Crisis in Pastoral Care," in *A History of Pastoral Care*, ed. G.R. Evans (London: Continuum, 2000), 228. Cornick goes on to state, "Luther's rediscovery of justification by faith spelt...a complete reordering of the way in which pastoral care was exercised" (229). See also Peter Brooks, "Martin Luther and the Pastoral Dilemma," in *Christian Spirituality: Essays in Honour of Gordon Rupp*, ed. Peter Brooks (London: SCM, 1975), 98–99.

[6] Martin Luther, "Ministers," in *What Luther Says: A Practical In-Home Anthology for the Active Christian*, ed. Ewald M. Plass (1959; repr., Saint Louis, MO: Concordia, 1994), 932. See chapter 1 for fuller quote.

went home and wrote a brief treatise on prayer for his barber! Luther opens with, "Dear Master Peter: I will tell you as best I can what I do personally when I pray. May our dear Lord grant to you and to everybody to do it better than I!" Luther directs him to the Psalms and other parts of Scripture to use in shaping his prayers.[7]

This was the concern of the Reformers, helping their people learn how to live and relate to God.[8] They knew they had rediscovered the life-giving gospel and were surrounded by people in desperate need of it.[9]

Next we can turn to Calvin, of whom it was said, "Though he may be first thought of as a theologian, he was even more a pastor of souls."[10] In 1538, the people of Geneva ran Calvin off; they kicked him out. The following year, the city received a letter from a Catholic archbishop urging them to return to Rome. Unable to respond, they sought out Calvin, the pastor they had rejected just the previous year. We might understand if, in such a situation, a pastor said, "Forget it! I'm not bothering with you. You didn't want me, remember?" But that was not Calvin's response. Instead

---

[7] Found in *Martin Luther's Basic Theological Writings*, ed. Timothy F. Lull and William R. Russell, 3rd ed. (Minneapolis, MN: Fortress, 2012), 33–38. This piece on prayer is a spiritual classic. See Carl R. Trueman: "A Lesson from Peter the Barber," *Themelios* 34 (2009): 3–5.

[8] "[T]he 'success' of his reform movement may in part be attributed to Luther's ability to meet the crisis of pastoral care caused by the medieval church's failure to address the spiritual needs of his contemporaries effectively." See Robert Kolb, "Luther the Master Pastor: Conrad Porta's *Pastorale Lutheri*, Handbook for Generations," *Concordia Journal* 9 (1983): 179.

[9] "[H]is proposals for liturgical renewal arose not merely out of speculation about what constituted 'correct evangelical worship' but out of care to see that the gospel was preached and celebrated in Wittenberg and among his dear Germans." See Timothy J. Wengert, "Introducing the Pastoral Luther," in *The Pastoral Luther: Essays on Martin Luther's Practical Theology*, ed. Timothy J. Wengert (Grand Rapids, MI: Eerdmans, 2009), 12. This book is an excellent resource for pursuing this topic further. For a moving account of the pastoral care given to and desired by Luther when he thought he was close to death see, Martin Lohrmann, "Bugenhagen's Pastoral Care of Martin Luther," *Lutheran Quarterly* 24:2 (Summer 2010): 125–136.

[10] J.D. Benoit, "Pastoral Care of the Prophet," in *John Calvin: Contemporary Prophet*, ed. Jacob Hoogstra (Grand Rapids, MI: Baker, 1959), 51.

he wrote a careful, pointed response, protecting Geneva and giving them ground to stand on:

> For though I am for the present relieved of the charge of the Church of Geneva, that circumstance ought not to prevent me from embracing it with paternal affection—God, when he gave it to me in charge, having bound me to be faithful to it forever. Now, then, when I see the worst snares laid for that Church, whose safety it has pleased the Lord to make my highest care, and grievous peril impending if not obviated, who will advise me to await the issue silent and unconcerned? How heartless, I ask, would it be to wink in idleness, and, as it were, vacillating at the destruction of one whose life you are bound vigilantly to guard and preserve? …assuredly I cannot cut off that charge any more than that of my own soul…my ministry (which, knowing it to be from Christ, I am bound, if need be, to maintain with my blood).[11]

This is no ivory-tower academician! This is a shepherd willing to spill his blood to protect his flock even when that flock despises his care for them.

Elsewhere, Calvin made this comment on pastoral care:

> We who have charge to teach the people must not only see what is profitable for them all in general, but we must also deal with everyone according to his age.
>
> But we must mark also, that it is not enough for a man who is a shepherd in the Church of God, to preach, and cast abroad the word into the air, we must have private admonitions also. And this is a point that many deceive themselves in. For they think that the order of the Church was made for no other end and purpose but that they should come to

---

[11] John Calvin, "Reply to Sadoleto," in *A Reformation Debate: John Calvin and Jacopo Sadoleto*, ed. John C. Olin (New York: Fordham University Press, 2000), 45.

Church one hour in the week, or certain days, and there hear a man speak, and when he has come out of the pulpit, he should hold his peace. Those who think so, show themselves sufficiently, that they never knew, either what Christianity, or God's order, meant.

For as we see in this passage...when he who has preached the word has taught the people, he must have an eye to those who have need to be warned of their faults privately.... And therefore, if we want to do our duty toward God, and to those who are committed to our charge, it is not enough for us to offer them the doctrine generally, but when we see any of them go astray, we must labor to bring him to the right way. When we see another in grief and sorrow, we must go about to comfort him. When we see anyone who is dull of the spirit, we must prick him and spur him, as his nature will bear.[12]

Calvin, and the other Reformers like him, was not an aloof preacher simply dispensing information.[13] They were shepherds involved in the everyday life of their people, seeing it as their task to help the people know God, pray, worship God, persevere and one day die well with the hope of the resurrection.[14] Calvin stated,

> Whatever others may think, we do not regard our office as bound within so narrow limits that when the sermon is delivered we may rest as if our task is done. They whose

---

[12] Sermon 37 in Ray Van Neste and Brian Denker, *John Calvin's Sermons on 1 Timothy* (CreateSpace, 2017), 144–145.

[13] Cornick demonstrates that Zwingli shared in this view: "The minister's work was not to be exhausted by preaching, for he must 'prevent the washed sheep falling into the excrement.'" See Cornick, "The Reformation Crisis," 235.

[14] Scott Manetsch has provided a comprehensive study of the pastoral work of the pastors in Geneva including Calvin and Theodore Beza in *Calvin's Company of Pastors: Pastoral Care and the Emerging Reformed Church, 1536–1609* (Oxford: Oxford University Press, 2013). See especially his chapter, "The Ministry of Pastoral Care."

blood will be required of us if lost through our slothfulness, are to be cared for much more closely and vigilantly.[15]

David Cornick states that contrary to the Catholic understanding of the confessional, in the ministry of Luther and his followers the work of dealing with sins "was transposed into the relationship of pastor and people, and a pulpit ministry grounded in a genuine knowledge of the congregation." As a result,

> The healing of souls was taken into the home. Visitation became a significant part of the pastor's life—especially to the sick, the dying and those in prison. As sacrificing priest became preaching minister, visitation became the locus of pastoral care.[16]

Theodore Beza exemplifies this in his sermon on John 21:15, where Jesus charged Peter, "Feed my sheep":

> It is not only necessary that [a pastor] have general knowledge of his flock, but he must also know and call each of his sheep by name, both in public and in their homes, both night and day. Pastors must run after lost sheep, bandaging up the one with a broken leg, strengthening the one that is sick.... In sum, the pastor must consider his sheep more dear to

---

[15] Cited in Wallace, *Calvin*, 173.
[16] Cornick, "The Reformation Crisis," 233. See also Manetsch, *Calvin's Company of Pastors*, 281; Wilhelm Pauck, "The Ministry in the Time of the Continental Reformation," in *The Ministry in Historical Perspectives*, ed. H. Richard Niebuhr and Daniel D. Williams (New York: Harper & Brothers, 1956), 110–147. Pauck writes, "There developed in Geneva, a regular practice of the care of souls. The Ordinances prescribed that each minister accompanied by an elder should regularly call in the homes of his parish. In 1550, an order was issued that the ministers should visit each home at least once a year. Beza commented on the effect of the order by saying, 'It is hard to believe how fruitful it proved to be'" (136). Pauck goes on to say other towns attempted this model of annual visitation but rarely accomplished it. Still, the other towns did expect regular visitation in the hospitals and prisons and of those sick and dying at home.

him than his own life, following the example of the Good Shepherd.[17]

Examples abound, but one clear place to see this is in the coming of the plague. People died at an alarming rate, and the showing of symptoms was regarded as a sign of death. Many fled the cities. But these men stayed at their posts. Twenty-five percent of the people in Zwingli's town died of the plague—and Zwingli was there ministering to them. He came down with the plague and almost died. When the plague came to Geneva and many fled, the pastors of Geneva met to ask who would visit the infected and care for them. Calvin volunteered, but the other ministers said they could not afford to lose him and held him back.[18]

This pastoral care can also be seen in the Reformers' counselling, which we have recorded in their voluminous correspondence.[19] One of Calvin's colleagues in Geneva wrote this of Calvin's pastoral ministry:

> No words of mine can declare the fidelity and prudence with which he gave counsel. The kindness with which he received all who came to him, the clearness and promptitude with which he replied to those who asked his opinion on the most important questions, and the ability with which he

---

[17] Cited in Manetsch, *Calvin's Company of Pastors*, 281.

[18] Theodore Beza, *The Life of John Calvin*, trans. Henry Beveridge (Philadelphia, PA: Westminster, 1909), 35. Writing to Viret, Calvin says he stands ready to take the place of the pastor who is visiting the plague victims if he gets sick. Calvin says he is in agreement with Viret that pastors cannot shirk this dangerous duty because their suffering people need them. He states, "As long as we are in this ministry, I do not see that any excuse will avail us if, through fear of infection, we are found wanting in the discharge of our duty where we are most needed." Cited in T.H.L. Parker, *Portrait of Calvin* (London: SCM Press, 1954), 81.

[19] See also John Knox's correspondence with his mother-in-law as she struggled with assurance of salvation, available in *The Select Practical Writings of John Knox* (Carlisle, PA: Banner of Truth, 2011). You've heard Knox thunder. Listen here as he comforts a tender soul with the balm of grace. Douglas Bond's brief, popular-level biography *The Mighty Weakness of John Knox* (Sanford, FL: Reformation Trust, 2011) is also helpful on this theme.

disentangled the difficulties and problems which were laid before him. Nor can I express the gentleness with which he could comfort the afflicted and raise the fallen and distressed.[20]

Calvin's correspondence is itself primary evidence of his pastoral heart, both in how many letters he took time to write and in how he wrote. Many of these letters had to do with diplomatic issues involving nations and the church at large. But as Ronald Wallace notes,

> even the diplomatic gives way entirely to an evangelistic motive and we find that his first concern is with his correspondent as a person. Is he or she keeping close to God, listening to his word continually, and likely to continue to resist the temptations of Satan in order to keep running well in the Christian race—in other words, how is it with your soul?[21]

In one letter, Calvin wrote to comfort a father who was grieving the death of his son, a student whom Calvin had known well. His letter opens with these words:

> When I first received intelligence of the death…of your son Louis, I was so utterly overpowered that for many days I was fit for nothing but to grieve; and albeit I was somehow upheld before the Lord by those aids wherewith he sustains our souls in affliction; among men, however, I was almost a nonentity.[22]

---

[20] Des Gallars, cited in Wallace, *Calvin*, 180–181.
[21] Wallace, *Calvin*, 170. Wallace's chapter, "The Pastor—The Cure of Souls," is very valuable. Wallace comments further, "Those who sought his counsel found in him, not only wisdom, but the strength that God often communicates to people through a trusted pastor" (*Calvin*, 181).
[22] Cited in the helpful essay by Robert Godfrey, "The Counselor to the Afflicted," in *John Calvin: A Heart for Devotion, Doctrine and Doxology*, ed. Burk

This is no fatalistic, unemotional response. Neither is it a lame, impotent response of an ivory-tower academic. Calvin, as a faithful pastor, begins with joining his friend's grief and then moves to sharing with this father the truths of God's providential care that bolstered his own soul. Calvin points to the son's faith in the gospel and the way it obviously impacted his life so that the father can hope for reunion in heaven.

After reminding the father of these grounds of comfort, Calvin returns to the reality of grief:

> Neither do I insist upon your laying aside all grief. Nor, in the school of Christ, do we learn any such philosophy as requires us to put off that common humanity with which God has endowed us, that, being men, we should be turned to stones.[23]

Another example of pastoral care is Martin Bucer, who was a mentor to Calvin. Bucer wrote *Concerning the True Care of Souls*, a significant treatise on pastoral ministry, in which, as I noted in chapter 1, his typical phrase for pastors is "carers for Souls."[24] His book is a gem, full of insight for the work of pastors.[25] His pastoral

---

Parsons (Orlando, FL: Reformation Trust, 2008), 88. Jean-Daniel Benoît also develops this theme further in his very helpful essay, "Pastoral Care of the Prophet," in *John Calvin: Contemporary Prophet: A Symposium*, ed. Jacob T. Hoogstra (Grand Rapids, MI: Baker, 1959). Benoit sates, "There was within him a humanity, a strength of sympathy, a warmth of soul, a pastoral concern which opened hearts to him" ("Pastoral Care of the Prophet," 67).

[23] Benoît, "Pastoral Care of the Prophet," 67.

[24] Martin Bucer, *Concerning the True Care of Souls*, trans. Peter Beale (Carlisle, PA: Banner of Truth, 2009). See also Bucer's comments on this theme in *De Regno Christi*, available in Wilhelm Pauck, ed., *Melanchthon and Bucer*, Library of Christian Classics (Louisville, KY: Westminster John Knox, 1969).

[25] Andrew Purves stated, "Martin Bucer's *On the True Pastoral Care (Von der waren Seelsorge)* is the principal Reformation text on pastoral theology" in *Pastoral Theology in the Classical Tradition* (Louisville, KY: Westminster John Knox, 2001), 76. It is "oriented to the practical care of souls," he writes. Purves lists high praise given to this book by leading historians, including J.T. McNeill, W.P. Stephens, David F. Wright and T.F. Torrance. Purves, like others, lamented that this book had not been translated into English and thus was little known

and evangelistic heart is seen throughout the book but especially in this lament:

> Where are the innocent servants of Christ who bring Christ's sheep nothing but the Lord's voice and word, who are zealous to seek all the Lord's lost sheep, to bring back those which have gone astray, to heal the injured, to strengthen the weak, to guard the strong and see them aright [Ezek. 34:16]?[26]

Bucer warns,

> Those ministers of Christ who abandon the baptized…will find it difficult to give account for them to God and Christ our Lord.… [T]he Lord will accuse these unreliable and unfaithful shepherds with great dismay: You have not searched for the lost [Ezek. 34:4].[27]

Bucer summarizes his aim with this comment: "Those who are ordained to the pastoral office in the church are to be the principal physicians of souls and guardians."[28]

2. Evangelism

Care for people naturally leads to a desire to see them reconciled to God and find forgiveness of their sins. Authentic pastoral care is always evangelistic, and this was also true for the Reformers. Examples of their evangelistic concern, labour and fervor abound, though I will provide only a few here.[29]

---

among non-specialists. With the fine new translation (cited above), this book seeks to redress this lack of awareness.

[26] Bucer, *Concerning the True Care of Souls*, xxxii.
[27] Bucer, *Concerning the True Care of Souls*, 89.
[28] Bucer, *Concerning the True Care of Souls*, 121.
[29] For similar sentiments in Zwingli, see "The Shepherd," in *In Search of True Religion: Reformation, Pastoral and Eucharistic Writings*, vol. 2 of *Selected Writings of Huldrych Zwingli*, trans. H. Wayne Pipkin (Allison Park, PA: Pickwick, 1984).

Contrary to the impression or assumption of many, Calvin exhibited this evangelistic concern.[30] *The Register of the Company of Pastors in Geneva* records numerous people sent out from Geneva during Calvin's time to "evangelize foreign parts." The records are incomplete, and eventually, due to persecution, it became too dangerous to record the names of those sent out, although it numbered more than 100 in one year alone. Philip Hughes notes that Geneva became a "school of missions" that had as one of its purposes

> to send out witnesses who would spread the teaching of the Reformation far and wide.... It [Geneva] was a dynamic centre of missionary concern and activity, an axis from which the light of the Good News radiated forth through the testimony of those who, after thorough preparation in this school, were sent forth in the service of Jesus Christ.[31]

In 1556 Calvin and his fellow ministers helped to support the first mission endeavour to target the New World, with a group sent to Brazil.[32] When you consider the lack of resources, the resistance, the persecution (each man sent out knew he was likely to be arrested, tortured and killed), this mission work is as impressive as anything we have to offer today.[33]

---

[30] Indeed, Benoît could state of Calvin, "From the outset his theological work is an effort of evangelization and of witnessing." See Benoît, "Pastoral Care of the Prophet," 51.

[31] *The Register of the Company of Pastors of Geneva in the Time of Calvin*, ed. and trans. Philip Hughes (Grand Rapids, MI: Eerdmans, 1966), 25.

[32] Cf. R. Pierce Beaver, "The Genevan Mission to Brazil," in *The Heritage of John Calvin*, ed. John H. Bratt (Grand Rapids, MI: Eerdmans, 1973), 55–73. Kenneth J. Stewart, "Calvinism and Missions: The Contested Relationship Revisited," *Themelios* 34 (2009): 63–78.

[33] See further, Philip E. Hughes, "John Calvin: Director of Missions," in *The Heritage of John Calvin*, ed. John H. Bratt (Grand Rapids, MI: Eerdmans, 1973), 40–54; Ray Van Neste, "John Calvin on Missions and Evangelism," *Founders Journal* 33 (1998): 15–21; Paul Helm, "Calvin, A.M. Toplady, and the Bebbington Thesis," in *The Advent of Evangelicalism: Exploring Historical Continuities*, ed.

Furthermore, Calvin's sermons reveal a pastor who regularly and earnestly urged his people to seek the salvation of the nations. In his sermons on 1 Timothy, Calvin regularly concludes with a prayer for the salvation of the nations. He calls on pastors to labour "mightily, and with greater zeal and earnestness" for the salvation of souls.[34] Even when people reject the salvation offered to them, Calvin tells pastors that they must continue to "take pains" in calling people to faith "and call as many to God as they can." Calvin urges, "we must take pains to draw all the world to salvation."[35]

As Calvin expounds Paul's call to pray "for all people" (1 Timothy 2:1), he applies this to our missionary responsibility to the world:

> Saint Paul's meaning in this place is to show us what the children of God ought to employ themselves in doing, and it is this, that we should not travail unprofitably, but instead call upon God and ask him to work toward the salvation of the whole world, and that we give ourselves to this work both night and day.[36]

Throughout this sermon Calvin calls for fervent prayer and persistent action for the salvation of souls. He tells his people, "the greatest pleasure we can do to men is to pray to God for them, and call upon him for their salvation."[37] In another sermon on 1 Timothy, Calvin also says every pastor must realize "that he is sent to go about the saving of souls, and therefore must give himself to it and be watchful therein, and take pains about it."[38]

Michael Haykin and Kenneth Stewart (Nashville, TN: Broadman & Holman, 2008), 205–208.

[34] Van Neste and Denker, *John Calvin's Sermons on 1 Timothy*, vol. 2, 133.
[35] Van Neste and Denker, *John Calvin's Sermons on 1 Timothy*, vol. 2, 141.
[36] Van Neste and Denker, *John Calvin's Sermons on 1 Timothy*, vol. 1, 156.
[37] Van Neste and Denker, *John Calvin's Sermons on 1 Timothy*, vol. 1, 159.
[38] Van Neste and Denker, *John Calvin's Sermons on 1 Timothy*, vol. 1, 293.

Lastly, we should once more consider Bucer. His book *Concerning the True Care of Souls* is filled with evangelistic pathos and exhortation. He even rebukes the church for failing to mount a more serious missionary endeavour to the "Jews and Turks" and says that the current threat from the Turks is God's judgement for their failure![39] Bucer calls for earnest, zealous evangelistic labour. To pastors he says, "true carers of souls and faithful ministers of Christ are not to miss anyone anywhere out with the word of salvation, but diligently to endeavour to seek out all those to whom they may have access in order to lead them to Christ our Lord."[40] Like Calvin, Bucer calls for perseverance in sharing the gospel with people who do not readily accept it: "faithful members of Christ are not to give up lightly on anyone."[41] In fact, Bucer says, "one should be so persistent with people [in calling them to faith] that to the evil flesh it seems to be a compulsion and urgent pressing."[42] For Bucer, zealous missionary work is rooted in God's desires and stirred by the example of Paul:

> He [God] desires that they should be sought wherever they are scattered, and sought with such seriousness and diligence that one should be ready to be all things to all men, as dear Paul was [1 Corinthians 9:22], and even to hazard one's own life, as the Lord himself did, so that the lost lambs might be found and won.[43]

Bucer affirmed God's sovereign election of souls to salvation, but did not see this as conflicting with energetic missionary enterprise:

---

[39] Bucer, *Concerning the True Care of Souls*, 87.
[40] Bucer, *Concerning the True Care of Souls*, 76.
[41] Bucer, *Concerning the True Care of Souls*, 78.
[42] Bucer, *Concerning the True Care of Souls*, 78.
[43] Bucer, *Concerning the True Care of Souls*, 78.

But it is not the Lord's will to reveal to us the secrets of his election; rather he commands us to go out into all the world and preach his gospel to every creature.... The fact that all people have been made by God and are God's creatures should therefore be reason enough for us to go to them, seeking with the utmost faithfulness to bring them to eternal life.[44]

Combining the pastoral care noted previously and evangelistic zeal, Bucer prayed,

> May the Lord Jesus, our chief Shepherd and Bishop, grant us such elders and carers of souls as will seek his lambs which are still lost, bring back those which have wandered, heal those which are wounded, strengthen those which are sickly, and guard and feed in the right way those which are healthy.[45]

This urgent, passionate call for evangelistic and missionary activity arises from a setting in which many of the men sent out as missionaries were killed. In one letter, Calvin addresses men who had been captured and imprisoned in Lyons for preaching the gospel. He had previously written and worked for their release. But once it was clear that all efforts had failed and their execution was imminent, Calvin wrote to encourage them to stand fast:

> Now, at this present hour, necessity itself exhorts you more than ever to turn your whole mind heavenward. As yet, we know not what will be the event. But since it appears as though God would use your blood to sign his truth, there is nothing better than for you to prepare yourselves to that end, beseeching him so to subdue you to his good pleasure, that nothing may hinder you from following whithersoever he

---

[44] Bucer, *Concerning the True Care of Souls*, 77.
[45] Bucer, *Concerning the True Care of Souls*, 193.

shall call.... You know, however, in what strength you have to fight—a strength on which all those who trust, shall never be daunted, much less confounded. Even so, my brothers, be confident that you shall be strengthened, according to your need, by the Spirit of our Lord Jesus, so that you shall not faint under the load of temptations, however heavy it be, any more than he did who won so glorious a victory, that in the midst of our miseries it is an unfailing pledge of our triumph. Since it pleases him to employ you to the death in maintaining his quarrel, he will strengthen your hands in the fight, and will not suffer a single drop of your blood to be spent in vain. And though the fruit may not all at once appear, yet in time it shall spring up more abundantly than we can express. But as he hath vouchsafed you this privilege, that your bonds have been renowned, and that the noise of them has been everywhere spread abroad, it must needs be, in despite of Satan, that your death should resound far more powerfully, so that the name of our Lord be magnified thereby. For my part, I have no doubt, if it please this kind Father to take you unto himself, that he has preserved you hitherto, in order that your long-continued imprisonments might serve as a preparation for the better awakening of those whom he has determined to edify by your end. For let enemies do their utmost, they never shall be able to bury out of sight that light which God has made to shine in you, in order to be contemplated from afar.[46]

Conclusion

This spirit of abandon for the sake of the gospel and the souls of people is the heritage of the Reformation, and we must maintain it.[47] Far from being unconcerned about gospel proclamation, the

---

[46] John Calvin, *Letters of John Calvin*, ed. Jules Bonnet (London: Hamilton, Adams, and Co., 1857), 2:387–388.

[47] For further reading on this topic, in addition to items already mentioned in the footnotes, see the following: R.W. Scribner, "Pastoral Care and the Reformation

example of these men is a strong challenge—even a rebuke—to us in our comfortable settings. Thus, the writings of the Reformers are of far more than antiquated or nostalgic interest. They are examples and goads to us today as we too seek to live out the gospel and advance Christ's kingdom in a fallen world. We dare not fail to learn from their successes and failures.

So, Christian, does the gospel animate your life, making you a person deeply concerned for and carefully aware of those around you? This example of our forebears calls us to this sort of faithfulness.

Young theologians, if your main activity is discussing theology but it does not result in a deep love and concern for people, you are no heir of the Reformation, regardless of your theological positions.

Pastors and those who desire to be pastors, if your idea of pastoral ministry is limited to the pulpit, then you are no heir of the Reformation regardless of the length or theological weight of your sermons. The Reformers, mirroring Christ and the apostles, were deeply involved in the lives of their people, aware that they would be called to account for the oversight of their souls.[48] A passion for souls requires the knowledge of specific souls and involvement in the messiness of their everyday lives.

---

in Germany," in *Humanism and Reform: the Church in Europe, England, and Scotland, 1400–1643: Essays in Honour of James K. Cameron* (Oxford: Blackwell, 1991), 77–97; Timothy J. Wengert, ed., *The Pastoral Luther: Essays on Martin Luther's Practical Theology* (Grand Rapids, MI: Eerdmans, 2009), especially Wengert, "Introducing the Pastoral Luther" (1–29); Theodore G. Tappert, ed., *Luther: Letters of Spiritual Counsel* (London: SCM, 1955)—Tappert's "General Introduction" is quite helpful; Pamela Biel, "Personal Conviction and Pastoral Care: Zwingli and the Cult of Saints 1522-1530," in *Zwingliana: Mitteilungen zur Geschichte Zwinglis der Reformation* 16 (1985): 442–469; Kenneth L. Parker, "Richard Greenham's 'Spiritual Physicke': The Comfort of Afflicted Consciences in Elizabethan Pastoral Care," in *Penitence in the Age of Reformations*, ed. Katharine Jackson Lualdi and Anne T. Thayer (London: Ashgate, 2000), 71–83.

[48] Hebrews 13:7.

3

Faithful pastoral ministry
and the "ministry of the Word"[1]

Introduction

Since the apostolic age, Acts 6:4 has been a seminal text for understanding the priorities of pastoral ministry. The dramatic growth of the early Jerusalem church precipitated a crisis for the apostles and their ministry. The needy widows of a minority group within the church (Greek-speaking Jews) were being neglected. In sorting out this problem, as Luke records in Acts 6, the apostles declared their two central and irreducible tasks:

---

[1] An earlier version of this essay appeared as "'Particular Medicine': Faithful Pastoral Ministry and τῇ διακονίᾳ τοῦ λόγου in Acts 6:4," in *God's Glory Revealed in Christ: Essays in Honor of Tom Schreiner*, ed. James Hamilton, Denny Burk, Brian J. Vickers (Nashville, TN: B&H Academic, 2019). Tom Schreiner exemplified well, for me, the private ministry of the Word argued for in this essay. In a challenging time in my life, he took time to meet with me and to help me sort through various ideas as I sought the will of God.

prayer and the ministry of the Word.[2] Recently, some Bible translators have rendered the Greek phrase τῇ διακονίᾳ τοῦ λόγου (literally, "the ministry of the Word") from Acts 6:4 as "preaching," "the preaching ministry" or similar phrases. Undoubtedly, the intention of these translations was to clarify or simplify a phrase thought to be ambiguous or complex. Translating the apostolic priorities in Acts 6:4 as "prayer and preaching,"[3] however, rather than the more common "prayer and ministry of the Word" is misleading. Something is lost in this interpretive simplification. The more literally rendered "ministry of the Word" connotes a broader semantic range than "preaching." For most contemporary English readers, "preaching" refers to ministry to the gathered church in public proclamation. However, when Paul describes his "ministry of the Word" among the Ephesian elders he says he taught them both "publicly and from house to house" (Acts 20:20).[4] The translation "preaching" in Acts 6:4 improperly limits the idea to public proclamation, which, I would argue, provides a basis for neglecting the private and personal ministry of the Word today.

To pursue this thesis, I will first examine the way Acts 6:4 has been translated across the spectrum of English translations. Such a survey demonstrates that the translation "preaching" is a more recent variation. Secondly, I will argue that the context of the rest of the book of Acts suggests a broader understanding of "ministry of the Word" than is connoted by "preaching" as understood by most English readers today. Third, I will illustrate how Acts 6:4,

---

[2] This mandate was in contrast to that of the newly formed group of "deacons" who would serve tables and meet the practical needs of the widows.

[3] Holman Christian Standard Bible (1999) has translated the phrase in this way. This has been changed to the traditional "prayer and ministry of the word" in the substantial revision of the translation published as the Christian Standard Bible (2017).

[4] This follows Luke's description of the apostles' activity prior to the crisis with the Grecian Jews. Acts 5:42 reads, "And every day, in the temple and from house to house, they did not cease teaching and preaching that the Christ is Jesus" (ESV). Luke's narrative and Paul's description follow the same formula.

particularly with the translation "preaching," affirms a view of pastoral ministry which is almost exclusively given to public proclamation. I will discuss the deleterious effects upon the church's ministry brought about by this understanding. Lastly, I will draw some implications from this study for our philosophy of translation.

Survey of English translations

In Acts 6:4 the phrase we are concerned with is τῇ διακονίᾳ τοῦ λόγου. The word διακονία is used by Luke and Paul to refer to serving others generally (Luke 10:40), specifically to meeting physical needs (Acts 11:29; 2 Corinthians 8:4; 9:1, 12) and to apostolic ministry (Romans 11:13; 2 Corinthians 4:1; 6:3; 1 Timothy 1:12). In Acts 6:1 the same word is used to refer to the daily distribution of food. This regular "ministry" of food distribution is delegated to the appointed seven men (the first deacons I believe),[5] while prayer and the "ministry" of the distribution of the "Word" will be the focus of the apostles.

Our concern here is what is meant by this "ministry of the Word." Is the *distribution of the Word* in view here limited to public proclamation? See Table 1 for a listing of some of the leading translations and how they render this verse.

The context of the book of Acts

The book of Acts provides further context for considering the scope of the "ministry of the Word" to which the apostles devoted themselves. First, Luke has already described the pattern of the apostles' teaching ministry in the previous chapter this way: "And every day, *in the temple and from house to house*, they did not cease

---

[5] J.B. Lightfoot states, "Universal tradition...connects the establishment of the 7 with the diaconate of later times." See *The Acts of the Apostles: A Newly Discovered Commentary*, ed. Ben Witherington III and Todd D. Still (Downers Grove, IL: IVP Academic, 2014), 106. Richard Pervo notes, "Since Irenaeus [*Against Heresies*] 1.26.3; 3.12.10; 4.15.1), followed by most of the tradition, this passage has been understood as the foundation of the diaconate." See *Acts: A Commentary* (Minneapolis, MN: Fortress, 2009), 161.

Table 1. Listing of how leading translations render Acts 6:4

"ministry of the word" (or equivalent)

King James Version	But we will give ourselves continually to prayer, and to the ministry of the word.
American Standard Version	But we will continue steadfastly in prayer, and in the ministry of the word.
Christian Standard Bible	But we will devote ourselves to prayer and to the ministry of the word.
Douay-Rheims American Edition	But we will give ourselves continually to prayer, and to the ministry of the word.
English Standard Version	But we will devote ourselves to prayer and to the ministry of the word.
Geneva Bible	And we will give ourselves continually to prayer, and to the ministration of the word.
Phillips New Testament	Then we shall devote ourselves whole-heartedly to prayer and the ministry of the Word.
Lexham English Bible	But we will devote ourselves to prayer and to the ministry of the word.
New American Standard Bible	But we will devote ourselves to prayer and to the ministry of the word.
New English Translation	But we will devote ourselves to prayer and to the ministry of the word.
New International Version	and will give our attention to prayer and the ministry of the word.
New King James Version	but we will give ourselves continually to prayer and to the ministry of the word.
New Revised Standard Version	while we, for our part, will devote ourselves to prayer and to serving the word.
Revised Standard Version	But we will devote ourselves to prayer and to the ministry of the word.

preaching (or equivalent)

Common English Bible	As for us, we will devote ourselves to prayer and the service of proclaiming the word.
Contemporary English Version	We can spend our time praying and serving God by preaching.
Good News Translation	We ourselves, then, will give our full time to prayer and the work of preaching.
Holman Christian Standard Bible	But we will devote ourselves to prayer and to the preaching ministry.
New Living Translation	Then we apostles can spend our time in prayer and teaching the word.*

*"Teaching the word" might be understood broadly enough to encompass more than pulpit ministry.

teaching and preaching that the Christ is Jesus" (Acts 5:42, emphasis added). This is simply a continuation of the practice of the church immediately following Pentecost where they met in the Temple and in homes (Acts 2:46). Thus, when "ministry of the Word" is mentioned in Acts 6 we should already be prepared to think of this as including public ministry (such as to crowds in the Temple) and private ministry, "from house to house."[6]

Alongside Acts 6:4, one of the most significant texts for pastoral ministry is Paul's description of his ministry to the Ephesians in Acts 20:17–35.[7] In this text Paul gives a farewell address to the pastors of the Ephesian church, summarizing his ministry among them as an example of proper ministry. Among other aspects of his ministry, Paul says he did not shrink back from declaring anything profitable, but he proclaimed to them the whole counsel of God. But where or in what context did this significant and comprehensive teaching ministry take place? He makes this explicit by stating that he taught them "in public and from house to house" (Acts 20:20). Thus, when Paul describes his teaching ministry, in an especially important setting where he is using his own labours as an example for other pastors, he makes the point of noting that his teaching ministry included both public *and* private teaching of the Word.[8]

On the significance of Paul's mention of both public and private ministry, Calvin[9] is worth quoting at length:

---

[6] Craig Keener also interprets these as marking public and private instruction. (Acts 2:12–44). Also Carl R. Holladay, *Acts: A Commentary* (Louisville, KY: Westminster John Knox Press, 2016), 149. See Keener further for discussion on the two verbs, *preaching* and *teaching*, as he demonstrates that they do not connote distinct activities but are used together to describe comprehensively the communication of God's message.

[7] David G. Peterson, *The Acts of the Apostles* (Grand Rapids, MI: Eerdmans, 2009), 234, points to Paul's message in Acts 20 as exemplifying what was meant by "ministry of the Word."

[8] Affirming that public and private is the sense here, see also, Eckhard J. Schnabel, *Acts*, Zondervan Exegetical Commentary on the New Testament (Grand Rapids, MI: Zondervan Academic, 2012), 840; Holladay, *Acts*, 397; Pervo, *Acts*, 520.

[9] Lest anyone believe Calvin was a pastor of a small, declining church, see

[Paul] did not only teach all men in the congregation, but also every one privately, as every man's necessity did require. For Christ hath not appointed pastors upon this condition, that they may only teach the Church in general in the open pulpit; but that they may take charge of every particular sheep, that they may bring back to the sheepfold those which wander and go astray, that they may strengthen those which are discouraged and weak, that they may cure the sick, that they may lift up and set on foot the feeble (Ezekiel 34:4), for common doctrine will oftentimes wax cold, unless it be helped with private admonitions.

Wherefore, the negligence of those men is inexcusable, who, having made one sermon, as if they had done their task, live all the rest of their time idly; as if their voice were shut up within the church walls, seeing that so soon as they be departed, thence they be dumb. Also, disciples and scholars are taught, that if they will be numbered in Christ's flock, they must give place to their pastors, so often as they come unto them; and that they must not refuse private admonitions. For they be rather bears than sheep, who do not vouchsafe to hear the voice of their pastor, unless he be in the pulpit; and cannot abide to be admonished and reproved at home, yea, do furiously refuse that necessary duty.[10]

Calvin reiterates this in his commentary on 1 Thessalonians 2:11:

It is not enough that a pastor in the pulpit teach all in common, if he does not add also particular instruction, according

---

Elsie Anne McKee's *The Pastoral Ministry and Worship in Calvin's Geneva* (Geneva: Droz, 2016) and Scott Manetsch's *Calvin's Company of Pastors: Pastoral Care and the Emerging Reformed Church, 1536–1609* (Oxford: Oxford University Press, 2013). Their study of the archival record of Geneva, both city and parish, make it clear that Calvin himself and his fellow pastors were much involved in active pastoral ministry (this included home visits and constant vigilance for the hundreds of souls in Geneva, as well as upward of 260 sermons preached each year by Calvin).

[10] John Calvin, *Commentary upon the Acts of the Apostles* (Grand Rapids, MI: Baker Books, 2003), 19:244.

as necessity requires, or occasion offers. Hence Paul himself, in Acts 20:26, declares himself to be *free from the blood of all men*, because he did not cease to admonish all publicly, and also individually in private in their own houses. For instruction given in common is sometimes of little service, and some cannot be corrected or cured without particular medicine.[11]

In fact, even in preaching on Acts 6, Calvin makes clear that private teaching is also in view, stating that God

> wants the charge kept inviolate until the end of the world so that preachers of the gospel will be able to accommodate the teaching according as they see a need and proclaim the word both in public and in private.[12]

Calvin's fellow reformer Martin Bucer also emphasizes the importance of private teaching, addressing Acts 20:26:

> Those pastors and teachers of the churches who want to fulfill their office and keep themselves clean of the blood of those of their flocks who are perishing should not only publicly administer Christian doctrine, but also announce, teach and entreat repentance toward God and faith in our Lord Jesus Christ, and whatever contributes toward piety…even at home and with each one privately.[13]

---

[11] John Calvin, *Commentary on the First Epistle to the Thessalonians* (Grand Rapids, MI: Baker Books, 2003) 21:254–255, emphasis added.

[12] John Calvin, *Sermons on the Acts of the Apostles: Chapters 1–7*, trans. Rob Roy McGregor (Edinburgh: Banner of Truth, 2008), 329. This can also be seen in Calvin's sermons on 1 Timothy, where preaching on 3:1–4, he says, "for a man to be a preacher, it is not a matter of one's sermon making, but he has to know that he must preach the word of God both publicly and privately, to edify and build up the people of God, that it may profit." See *John Calvin's Sermons on 1 Timothy*, vol. 1, ed. Ray Van Neste and Brian Denker (CreateSpace, 2017), 295.

[13] Martin Bucer, *De Regno Christi*, in *Melanchthon and Bucer*, ed. Wilhelm Pauck (Philadelphia: The Westminster Press, 1969), 235.

More recently, Paul Beasley-Murray assessed the apostle Paul's work as a pastor like this:

> Paul was concerned not just for the corporate health of the churches in his care, but also for the well-being of individuals. People mattered to Paul.... In 1 Thessalonians 2:11 Paul declared: "We dealt with each one of you like a father with his children," implying that he had concerned himself with his converts on an individual basis. Similarly, Paul emphasized the personal character of his work in Colossians 1:28: he sought to promote individual maturity by "warning and teaching everyone in all wisdom." All this is in line with Luke's account of Paul's speech to the Ephesian elders, which suggests that his normal practice was to combine preaching to the church at large together with the visiting of individual church members (Acts 20:20).[14]

In the context of the book of Acts it becomes clear that the apostolic priority of "the ministry of the Word" cannot be limited to public proclamation. With this conclusion in view, let us return to the range of terms used in English translations. The literal "ministry of the Word" leaves open the possibility of private and public proclamation. "Teaching" or "speaking God's Word" are both also likely to be understood as potentially involving public and private settings. However, "preaching" (CEV) or "preaching ministry" (HCSB) is likely to be understood only in terms of public ministry.[15]

---

[14] P. Beasley-Murray, "Paul as Pastor." In *Dictionary of Paul and His Letters*, eds. Gerald F. Hawthorne, Ralph P. Martin, and Daniel G. Reid (Downers Grove, IL: InterVarsity, 1993), 657.

[15] See Peter Adam's excellent book on preaching, *Speaking God's Words: A Practical Theology of Expository Preaching* (Downers Grove, IL: IVP, 1996), especially chapter four, "Preaching as *a* ministry of the Word" (emphasis added).

Problematic implications for pastoral ministry

The Christian church, generally, has historically understood pastors to be carrying on the apostles' work, especially their ministerial labours in prayer and the Word. As I teach pastoral ministry or speak to pastors about their labours, I seek to counter the idea that public ministry is the sum of pastoral ministry. Chapter 1 of this book contains my effort, drawing from numerous New Testament texts and historical examples, to argue that *the soul of pastoral work is the oversight of souls*, which includes but goes well beyond preaching. I argue for the necessity of pastoral visitation, keeping up with the needs and spiritual state of your congregants. In such settings, someone will typically point to Acts 6:4 as a text which seems to contradict what I am saying. "But didn't the apostles just devote themselves to prayer and preaching?" The answer is no, they did not, at least not if by "preaching" you mean simply public proclamation. I point them to Acts 20:20, as I have discussed above, but translating "ministry of the Word" in Acts 6:4 as "preaching" or "preaching ministry" short circuits such a conversation. The reader is unwittingly prevented from thinking of the *ministry of the Word* in any broader terms. When we already have cultural currents pushing us away from the private side of pastoral ministry, the last thing we need is translations that obscure it.

Julia Duin, cited in chapter 1, documented the fallout in our churches when people do not feel like they are being pastored, but are simply expected to attend mass meetings.[16] This problem has only increased since that book was published. One of the most common complaints I hear from churches is that their pastors preach but do not engage members personally or care for them in person in times of crises or trial. Yet, the leading voices from our past remind us of the importance of such care. For example, Theodore Cuyler stated:

---

[16] Julia Duin, *Quitting Church: Why the Faithful Are Fleeing and What To Do About It* (Grand Rapids, MI: Baker, 2009), 22–23.

Let a pastor make himself at home in everybody's home; let him come often and visit their sick rooms, and kneel beside their empty cribs, and their broken hearts, and pray with them; let him go to the businessmen in his congregation when they have suffered reverses and give them a word of cheer; let him be quick to recognize the poor, and the children—and he will weave a cord around the hearts of his people that will stand a prodigious pressure. His inferior sermons—(for every minister is guilty of such occasionally)—will be kindly condoned, and he can launch the most pungent truths at his auditors and they will not take offense. He will have won their hearts to himself, and that is a great step towards drawing them to the house of God, and winning their souls to the Savior. "A house-going minister" said Chalmers, "makes a church-going people."[17]

Certainly, the celebrity culture, which has infected even the church, does not help us here. Individual work with people cannot be seen or distributed and, thus, does not promote "a platform." As Calvin Miller stated, "No one ever gets his or her picture in an evangelical magazine simply because they visited the sick."[18] People are messy and individual work is complicated, tangled and slow. But, as Cuyler said, "Every pulpit needs to be vitalized by close contact with living people."[19]

The implications of the broader *ministry of the Word* are missed far too often. We need the breadth of this ministry highlighted, not obscured by translation. Individualized ministry is the norm across the New Testament, even if we are conditioned today by experience to miss it. Below are just a few examples.

In Colossians 1:28, where Paul summarizes his ministry, he states, "[Christ] we proclaim, warning everyone and teaching

---

[17] Cuyler, *How To Be a Pastor*, 2–3. Thomas Chalmers (1780–1847) was a Scottish Presbyterian pastor and professor.

[18] Calvin Miller, *O Shepherd, Where Art Thou?* (Nashville, TN: B&H, 2006), 42.

[19] Cuyler, *How To Be a Pastor*, 3.

everyone with all wisdom, that we may present everyone mature in Christ." Paul is not focused simply on a large crowd but is concerned for his teaching to reach and shape each member of the congregation. Commenting on Paul's repeated use of "everyone" here, Peter O'Brien states, "The singular is used to show that each person individually...was the object of the apostle's care."[20]

The apostle Peter, speaking to other pastors writes,

> So I exhort the elders among you, as a fellow elder and a witness of the sufferings of Christ, as well as a partaker in the glory that is going to be revealed: *shepherd the flock of God that is among you,* exercising oversight, not under compulsion, but willingly, as God would have you; not for shameful gain, but eagerly (1 Peter 5:1–2; emphasis added).

The key command here is to shepherd, which cannot be reduced to sermons from afar. Sermons play a key role, but they do not exhaust the work of the pastoral office. The use of shepherd imagery is rooted in the work and example of Jesus as the Great Shepherd (cf. Hebrews 13:20), who said:

> I am the good shepherd. The good shepherd lays down his life for the sheep. He who is a hired hand and not a shepherd, who does not own the sheep, sees the wolf coming and leaves the sheep and flees, and the wolf snatches them and scatters them. He flees because he is a hired hand and cares nothing for the sheep. I am the good shepherd. I know my own and my own know me, just as the Father knows me and I know the Father; and I lay down my life for the sheep (John 10:11–15).

Lastly, and perhaps most significantly, Hebrews 13:17 summarizes the pastoral role, stating that pastors "are keeping watch

---

[20] Peter O'Brien, *Colossians, Philemon* (Waco, TX: Word Books, 1982), 88.

over your souls, as those who will have to give an account." It is hard to imagine this accounting as being anything other than individual and particular. If we must give account for each one, we surely must minister to each one in addition to speaking to the whole congregation. It will be difficult to give account to God for souls whose names we do not know.

This is a significant aspect of ministry, significant in terms of the impact on people, its importance to kingdom growth and the percentage of a pastor's time it will take. We ought not to have pastors in training thinking that the sum of their labours will be preaching and sermon preparation. We are setting them up for failure and setting our churches up for harm. This line of thinking impoverishes preaching, as the pastor lacks the close knowledge of his people required in order to apply the text most helpfully, most graciously and most directly. John Angell James stated well, "He who can only generalize in the pulpit, but has not ability to individualize out of it—may be a popular preacher, but he is little fitted to be the pastor of a Christian church."[21] As Peter Adam has stated,

> Those of us who are committed to preaching need to be committed to a wider ministry of the Word as well. We need to see preaching as part of that ministry of the Word. Otherwise we shall try to make preaching do what it cannot easily achieve. Not only will God's people suffer because they do not receive other ministries of the Word, but our preaching will suffer as we force it into an alien mould. Our ministry may be pulpit-centered, but it should not be pulpit-restricted, for such a ministry of the Word will suffer severe limitations.[22]

---

[21] John Angell James, *An Earnest Ministry: The Want of Our Times* (Carlisle, PA: Banner of Truth, 1993), 151.
[22] Adam, *Speaking God's Words*, 74–75.

And so, translations which render τῇ διακονίᾳ τοῦ λόγου simply as "preaching" (or its equivalent) obscure this point. They prevent people from seeing this component of a pastor's work, helping pastors to overlook this work and helping church members miss an aspect of ministry they should expect.

Conclusion: Implications for translation work

What then are the implications for the way we approach Bible translation? Of course, there is no strictly literal translation. Interpretation is always in view. But we must be careful not to *over* interpret. We must be very careful that our well-intended clarifications do not obscure connections elsewhere in the text. Of course, there will be difficult decisions and balancing acts, but I believe it will be safer to err on the side of literal, even allowing people to wrestle with some ambiguity. As Anthony Esolen has stated well:

> So the biblical language is sometimes strange. Let it be. So people do not always understand it. The better then to suggest to them that in fact they do not understand it, and that there are mysteries whose surfaces they have only begun to peer into.[23]

We ought not make interpretive decisions for the reader unnecessarily, and we ought not assume they are not up for some wrestling. This is an all too common mistake when the goal is for the "person on the street" to be able to understand the text on their own. This completely misses the need for the teaching function of the church. There is a basic level of understanding, but we ought to expect any translation of the Bible to have rough edges, difficult portions—precisely because the original has these!—which will require much thought and should drive us to

---

[23] Anthony Esolen, "Word to the Wise," in "Quodlibet," *Touchstone: Journal of Mere Christianity* 19:6 (December 2006): 5.

the teachers God has given to the church (Ephesians 4:11–12). We do want clarity in translations, but we do not want simplification which removes the opportunity to see broader aspects of what is in view. In some cases, like this one in Acts 6:4, the restriction of interpretive options is harmful.

Portrait of a faithful, approved workman
An exhortation to seminarians (2 Timothy 2:14–26)[1]

Introduction

I do not know what the Lord has called you to do. I hope many of you are in seminary because the Lord is calling you to pastoral ministry. It is a need our land cries out for today. Yet, there is

---

[1] An earlier version of this essay published as "Portrait of a Faithful, Approved Workman: An Exhortation to Seminarians, 2 Timothy 2:14-26," *Criswell Theological Review* 20:1 (Fall 2022): 107–118. It was originally given during the Biblical Studies Lectures at Beeson Divinity School, February 11–13, 2020. I am grateful to Timothy George for the original invitation and to Douglas Sweeney for his gracious hospitality and encouragement. An earlier version was given at California Baptist University as part of their School of Christian Ministries Lecture series, April 5, 2018.

confusion in the church about what pastoral ministry is. Too often I hear people critique their pastor, sounding like sports fans complaining that their quarterback has not thrown a complete game or has no strikeouts. If we heard someone speak like this, we would think they had wrong expectations because they were confusing two different games. But this is exactly what I think when I hear people talk about pastors. Back in 1990, John Stott (1921–2011) wrote,

> In our day, in which there is much confusion about the nature and purpose of the pastoral ministry and much questioning whether the clergy are primarily social workers, psychotherapists, educators, facilitators or administrators, it is important to rehabilitate the noble word "Pastors" who are shepherds of Christ's sheep, called to tend, feed and protect them.[2]

Stott was right. We cannot appreciate the significance of pastoral ministry without reckoning with what is at stake in shepherding God's people. This is not to elevate what some people do in the body of Christ over others. We are simply acknowledging that pastoring is a weighty task. So much so, it is why Paul—in his letters where he talks about pastoral ministry—uses words like *labour*, *struggle*, *toil* and *hardship*. It should not surprise us, then, when we encounter adversity along the way in ministry. Regarding this point, I commend to you a wonderful and powerful sermon from the seventeenth century by Henry Scougal, a Scottish pastor and professor at the University of Aberdeen. In his sermon, he said,

> And shall we undervalue the price of His blood or think it a small matter to have the charge of those for whom it was shed? It is the Church of God we must oversee and feed, the Church for which the world is upheld, which is sanctified by

---

[2] John Stott, *The Message of Acts* (Downers Grove, IL: Intervarsity, 1990), 323.

the Holy Ghost on which the angels themselves attend. What a weighty charge is this that we have undertaken! And who is sufficient for these things?[3]

Such sage words serve as a nice segue to introduce the text I want to share with you about the pastoral task, a passage where Paul offers some of his final words to a young son in the faith.

Paul's words in 2 Timothy 2

In Paul's last letter, the apostle writes to Timothy about issues in the church at Ephesus. A transition occurs in the letter at 2 Timothy 2:14–26 where Paul shifts to speaking directly to Timothy about his pastoral task. So let us examine this text to see three crucial aspects that describe the character of a man who would serve as pastor:

1. Approved by God (2:14–18)
2. A holy man (2:19–23)
3. A patient teacher (2:24–26)

1. Approved by God (2 Timothy 2:14–18)

[14] Remind them of these things, and charge them before God not to quarrel about words, which does no good, but only ruins the hearers. [15] Do your best to present yourself to God as one approved, a worker who has no need to be ashamed, rightly handling the word of truth. [16] But avoid irreverent babble, for it will lead people into more and more ungodliness, [17] and their talk will spread like gangrene. Among them are Hymenaeus and Philetus, [18] who have swerved from the truth, saying that the resurrection has already happened. They are upsetting the faith of some (2 Timothy 2:14–18).

---

[3] Henry Scougal, "The Importance and Difficulty of the Ministerial Function," in *The Works of the Rev. Henry Scougal*, ed. Don Kistler (1765; repr. Morgan, PA: Soli Deo Gloria, 2002), 234.

This paragraph is arranged with a negative (v. 14), a positive (v. 15) and a subsequent negative (vv. 16–18). What Paul says Timothy should do is sandwiched between types of behaviour he is told to avoid.

We begin with the positive, which is the call to seek God's approval (v. 15). It may be that few of you had the privilege of growing up with Bible Drill as I did. Bible Drill (or Sword Drill) was a denominational program engaging children and youth in the systematic memorization and location of Scripture. When we received our official Bible Drill Bibles, they had 2 Timothy 2:15 inscribed on the front cover: "Study to show thyself approved" (KJV). Modern translations rightly do not use the word *study* because the original Greek verb does not refer to what we mean by *study* today.[4] Still, this verse is often used to call for faithful handling of God's Word. That is a proper use of this verse, which I will address momentarily, but I think we often miss this first command in the verse.

I remember where I was when the verb in this verse first grabbed my attention and shook me. It was early in my ministry and I was studying this passage with my Greek text and English translations in my basement study. I had become accustomed to reading Paul's command as "Do your best" (cf. ESV, NIV, RSV), but I stared at the verb σπουδάζω, knowing that this was too sleepy a translation. It is not heretical, and I can see what the translators were after originally. Still, where in our cultural setting do we use the phrase, "Do your best"? I think of a mother with a child heading to take a test at school. The child is worried she may not do well, and the mother says, "Just do your best, dear." Or one may envision someone who does not quite succeed in a task, and they console themselves by saying, "I did my best." In too many cases, functionally, "Do your best" simply means, "Give it a try, and it is okay if you do not succeed." Yet that is not the meaning

---

[4] The KJV rendering was accurate in the 1600s, but our use of the word *study* has changed over time.

of this word, especially in this context. Rather, the term means to *be zealous in the pursuit of something*, to take pains to accomplish an objective.[5] Some translations get closer with "be diligent" (NASB, CSB), but there is still more to it. The idea of the word is that we should be captivated by zealous pursuit of the approval of God. So, in my basement that evening, I wrote down this question to which I regularly return: "Is my life marked by a wholehearted pursuit of the approval of God?" Is the number one goal in my life to reach the final day when everything else is done and I stand before God the Father Almighty, Maker of heaven and earth, to hear him say those words, "Well done, good and faithful servant." What could be more significant?

Admittedly, I do not live that way enough. Far too often, I am more captivated by hearing people tell me I have done well in my pastoral duties and preaching. Even the desire for the praise of people I do not know can easily rank higher in my heart than the Lord's approval. Of course, wanting to be on good terms with others is a good thing. Sometimes I hear people say, "I do not care what anybody thinks," to which I want to say, "Then you are a sociopath." It is not that we are apathetic about how others feel about us. The issue is *priority*. What animates or motivates you? What grips your soul to the extent that you are willing to say, "If everything else must be lost, to this I will hold"?

If nobody praises us, if we die with people slandering our name and others believing the slander, if we die having seen precious little progress of the gospel in our ministries, and yet we hear God say, "Well done, good and faithful servant," it will all be worth it. All the slander and unfounded critiques of people will mean nothing. However, if we end this life vaunted on the praise and celebration of the whole world and fail to hear those words, none of it will matter.

---

[5] Walter Bauer, *A Greek-English Lexicon of the New Testament and Other Early Christian Literature*, trans. William F. Arndt and F. Wilbur Gingrich, rev. Frederick William Danker, 3rd ed. (Chicago, IL: University of Chicago Press, 2000), s.v., 3, 939.

This is what Paul is saying as he approaches the end of his days and reaches out to his young protégé Timothy. Paul says, "Be earnest, be zealous to present yourself to God as one who receives approval." This is what it is all about. This is the task. If we are captivated by this, we will begin to say, "How do we get there? How do we pursue this goal?"

Yet before moving to the how, we should linger here because the chief obstacle to living for the praise of God is living for the praise of man. Surely, you have noticed this in Scripture, the praise of man and the fear of man go together just like the praise of God and the fear of God.

In popular culture, a common statement you find on T-shirts and other items is, "Fear no one." This is either a dishonest or foolish claim because you are created in such a way that you will fear someone—the only question is will you fear people or God? Will you live for the praise of people or will you live for the praise of God?

Related to this point, I am captivated by a couple of Jesus' statements in the Gospel of John. In John 12:43, Jesus rebukes certain people as those who love the glory that comes from man more than the glory that comes from God. Even more startling, in John 5:44, Jesus says, "How can you believe, when you receive glory from one another and do not seek the glory that comes from the only God?" Jesus suggests you cannot even believe if you seek the glory that comes from man. Seeking the glory of man fights against faith. So, we must turn away, and seek zealously this approval from God alone.

How, then, do we pursue such heavenly approval? The answer begins in 2 Timothy 2:14 where Paul reminds Timothy (and us) not to quarrel about words that bring no good and cause only ruin to the hearers. Verse 16 says "avoid irreverent babble," which are meaningless arguments about words. This is a particular temptation to a divinity school community.

Paul is not saying here that *all* words are arbitrary. This is the same Paul who rebuked Peter at Galatia when his actions involving Jewish and Gentile believers compromised a central concept of the gospel encapsulated by one word—*alone*. This is Paul's emphatic claim in Galatians. These believers were not being told to doubt they were saved by Christ. It was just that their faith in Christ needed to be supplemented by compliance to certain Old Testament demands. Paul's counter, however, was that they were saved by Christ alone. So while no one doubted faith in Christ was *essential*, Paul insisted faith alone was *sufficient*.

Therefore, while words do matter, not every argument about every word does. There are meaningless arguments, many online, and it is easy, as you begin to learn the truths of the Scriptures and theology, to move into argumentativeness. This contentiousness or combativeness can sometimes unite with a desire for the praise of man, gradually causing us to ride forth on what we think is our great steed of righteousness. Yet it is a puny pony because we merely look for arguments to conquer, chances to showcase who we think we are and proclaim to the world what we think we can contribute to the kingdom.

To such antics, our text says, "Stop it." Remember, not every dispute out there needs *your* voice. Sometimes this is hard to hear. Let me even say it this way, "You are not ready to take on every dispute out there." None of us are. Your responsibility is to give your energy to the place where you are connected. The question to ask is, to whom do you have responsibility? Where are your connections? Where is your service? You can begin to find answers to these questions by looking at the circle(s) within your local church. Many of your obligations begin there. Along the way, the Lord may also put you in places where you need to speak publicly about something. There are divinely appointed times for such occasions, and we do need people who can step up in those moments. But it is not for everybody, especially those who are not ready. None of us should think we are up to those challenges if we are being unfaithful to clear responsibilities right in front of us.

This is why I tell pastors to keep their heads down and focus on matters most pertinent to the people they shepherd. Be aware of what is going on in your own churches. Know how your people are doing. Be sensitive to the issues they are facing. If we are honest, sometimes we can be tempted to think what our people are dealing with is not nearly as exciting as what is out there. When we begin entertaining thoughts like this, it does not take long to see where such bad thinking can lead.

So again, "avoid irreverent babble." Do not get caught up in it. It is appealing—especially online—but it is a trap. Turn away and look to Paul's point in verse 15. The zealous pursuit of God's approval requires us to heed Paul's call to centre on rightly handling the Word of truth. We do this as good students by constantly training and disciplining ourselves to handle the Word of God correctly. Be mindful that it is easier to be distracted by irreverent babble than staying focused on knowing the Word and being shaped by it.

To encourage you on this point, hear a few exhortations from our past heroes as they urge us in the right direction. Hear Charles Spurgeon who says, "Ah, beloved. Let us thank God for the Bible. Let us love it. Let us count it more precious than much fine gold."[6] You have heard numerous admonitions like this one to affirm God's truth. I am sure you believe them, but I want to press you to continue *living* that truth. While you may know it is something to affirm, it may not be something that consumes you as it should. Here, Richard Baxter is helpful when he exhorts, "So I warn you, as you love your souls, keep close to Scripture and to the faithful ministry of the Word." Baxter again says, "Then let able faithful men be the overseers who make the Word of God their rule. If only would-be leaders of the church might be contented with a sufficient Word of God and not impose new

---

[6] Charles Haddon Spurgeon, "The Bible," in *The New Park Street Pulpit*, vol. 1 (Grand Rapids, MI: Baker Book House, 1990), 112.

canons and authorities over it."[7] Or hear Charles Brown who exclaimed,

> Oh, if you would preach well, acquaint yourselves, I beseech you, with this blessed volume. Literally get it by heart; delight much in it; learn to say of it, "I rejoice at Thy word, as one that findeth great spoil" (Ps 119:162)—"Thy words were found, and I did eat them; and Thy word was unto me the joy and rejoicing of mine heart" (Jer 15:16). Strive to be able to quote Scripture with ease, and with accuracy.[8]

Along this line, I recounted earlier about being brought up doing Bible Drill. Many of the Scriptures I memorized as a child are the first ones that still come to my mind. Nonetheless, it was while I was at seminary that some well-meaning friends began to snipe at Scripture memory. "Do you know the whole context of that verse you just memorized? Did you memorize the whole chapter? No? Well, what good is it? Did you memorize it in Greek or Hebrew? No? Well, what good is it?" Even though I remain unaware of their overall intention for this barrage of questioning, the sad result was that I eventually stopped memorizing Scripture— and I deeply regret that decision.

How foolish it was for students at a seminary to denigrate the memorization of the very words of life. So, I implore those who are in seminary to avoid this attitude and train for the ministry of the Word. Let it sink into your hearts. Let it grip your souls now because you are training to go out into a broken and fallen world that desperately needs answers. You are also being pressed by the world around you to use other tools for ministry. Yet all of them are worthless without the foundation of God's Word.

---

[7] Richard Baxter, *The Reformed Pastor*, ed. James M. Houston (Portland, ME: Multnomah, 1982), 9, 11.

[8] Charles J. Brown, *The Ministry: Addresses to Students of Divinity* (Carlisle, PA: Banner of Truth, 2006), 47–48.

This will prove to be true in the future when you find yourself in moments where the lives of others are falling apart. People will look to you and say, "Pastor, what do you have to say?" Whether they know it or not, what they are really asking is, "What does *God* say?" You will need to have the Word ready to share. In those moments, it will often be intimidating because you will second-guess yourself when these circumstances expose your shortcomings and lack of wisdom. But in these situations, just know that who you are is irrelevant. What God says is what counts. Learn the Word of God. Memorize it. Give yourself to your studies. Paul says to do this "so you need not to be ashamed." The implication is that you will be shamed if you cannot rightly handle the Word of God. Thus, always be aware that this is why you are in seminary, to learn. Make the most of it. To encourage you, let me quote Scougal once more at some length.

> But if the negligence and miscarriage of a minister hazards the souls of others, it certainly ruins his own; which made St. Chrysostom say (words so terrible that I tremble to put them into English), "If a man should speak fire, blood, and smoke; if flames could come out of his mouth instead of words; if he had a voice like thunder and an eye like lightning, he could not sufficiently represent the dreadful account that an unfaithful pastor shall make. What horror and confusion shall it cast them into at the last day to hear the blood of the Son of God plead against them, to hear our great Master say, 'It was the purchase of My blood which ye did neglect! God died for these souls, of whom ye took so little pains!' Think not, therefore, to be saved by that blood which ye have despised, or to escape the torments whereunto many others are plunged through your faults!" By this time, I hope it appears that the work of the ministry is of great weight and importance; that much depends on the right discharging of

it, and that miscarrying in it is the most dangerous thing in the world.⁹

While this may sound excessive today in our indifferent age, we ought to hear Scougal as one who was earnest for souls. He reminds us about the careful discharging of gospel ministry and how miscarrying our mission is the most dangerous thing in the world. We must feel the weight of this. Those in seminary need to let the gravity of this task shape them during their studies. It is imperative to do this because you are not attending seminary to play games. You did not come to seminary to dally with doctrine or banter about belief. You came to toil for truth.

This is why I am troubled when I occasionally hear students who express sentiments like, "Many of the people I know are not really interested in theology or doctrine. And I just want to love them and give them the help they can understand." In response, I would remind you it is not without reason the church, since the fourth century at least, has referred to pastors as "physicians of souls." So, ask yourself, do you want a doctor for your body who in his training said, "Listen, my patients aren't worried about all these complicated words, about diseases and body parts—femur, fibula, thyroid, thorax, whatever. I just want to help people"? Of course not! You want doctors who know all these things. You want medical practitioners who know the latest about different illnesses, who understand the technical terms about cutting-edge procedures and medicines, and who can convey all this information clearly in terms a patient can understand. Moreover, the fact that we do not see the same dynamics applying to those who serve as the physicians of our souls shows how misguided our priorities are.

If God is pleased to place you in pastoral ministry, it is so you can care for souls, which he purchased with his own blood (Acts 20:28). Therefore, you need at least as good a preparation for this

---

⁹ Scougal, "The Importance and Difficulty of the Ministerial Function," 235.

noble calling as you would for caring for bodies. Additionally, be mindful that the educational opportunity before you is the envy of the world today. It would even be the envy of Christians across the ages. So hear me: you dare not yawn at it. No class is just another hurdle to endure. Your Greek parsing, Hebrew vocabulary, historical and theological analysis—all this work is expected so you might *know* the Word of God to *help* the people of God. This is the mission entrusted to you as you venture out into the broken world. You are to help those who are hurting by bringing God's Word to bear on their struggles —because it is effective and up to the task.

Something so powerful must be used with great discretion. It must be handled properly and as our text says, this is what you are training to do. You are preparing yourself to handle God's Word carefully and one day hear God himself say, "Well done." To experience this, you must know that devotion to God's Word *now* will help shape what things will look like at the *end* of your race. So, give yourself to the Word of God.

2. A holy man (2 Timothy 2:19–23)

> [19] But God's firm foundation stands, bearing this seal: "The Lord knows those who are his," and, "Let everyone who names the name of the Lord depart from iniquity."
>
> [20] Now in a great house there are not only vessels of gold and silver but also of wood and clay, some for honorable use, some for dishonorable. [21] Therefore, if anyone cleanses himself from what is dishonorable, he will be a vessel for honorable use, set apart as holy, useful to the master of the house, ready for every good work.
>
> [22] So flee youthful passions and pursue righteousness, faith, love, and peace, along with those who call on the Lord from a pure heart. [23] Have nothing to do with foolish, ignorant controversies; you know that they breed quarrels.

Paul's next exhortation pertains to holiness. It is offered in the context of disruption in the church as false teachers were leading people astray. Paul reminds Timothy that God's work is secure: "God's firm foundation stands." Then he says the foundation of God's church has a seal, which draws from two Old Testament texts (Numbers 16:5; Isaiah 26:13). Paul's overall point is no matter what someone sees in a local church, God's work is sure because it retains a two-part seal: "The Lord knows those who are his" and "Let everyone who names the name of the Lord depart from iniquity."

Notice that divine sovereignty and human responsibility are both found in this seal. First, consider *divine sovereignty*: the Lord knows those who are his. It is critical to recognize this as you minister: there will be people who profess faith only later to wander away from it. It will tear at your heart, yet you must remember the Lord knows his own. You and I are often going to be surprised in ministry—but rest assured the Lord is not. He is secure and we are secure in him.

The second part of the seal stresses personal holiness with the claim, "Let everyone who names the name of the Lord depart from iniquity." Paul develops this point further by using a house as a metaphor. In a normal house, you would probably have wood or clay vessels. However, in a rich house, you would have more valuable vessels of gold or silver. Paul says, "If anyone cleanses himself from what is dishonorable, he will be a vessel for honorable use" (v.21). This is an appeal: "Cleanse yourself!" In context, he means be cleansed both from sin and from false teaching so you might be a vessel for honourable use in the hand of the Lord—"useful to the master." Indeed, this phrase should be what our hearts long for. We should yearn to hear the Lord say, "This one is useful."[10]

These words imply that God is holding forth two options. You can either be a golden goblet or a vessel of dishonour. I implore

---

[10] This is precisely what Paul says about Mark later in 2 Timothy 4:11.

you to keep yourself clean so you can always be an honourable vessel that the Master can use.

Paul adds that part of the means for maintaining this kind of purity is to "flee youthful passions." We typically think of sexual sin when we read this phrase. Yet it is not limited to this idea. There are significant scholarly discussions about what all is involved here, with some suggesting that Paul has the pursuit of novelty in mind,[11] or impatience and eagerness for arguing.[12] At the very least, he is saying that we must be serious about combatting sin, chasing after holiness and allowing godly people to help us in these endeavours.

One sin that I think tends to stifle this process and fester in the seminary setting is pride. While it is not unique to youth, it can flourish when immature eagerness for dispute and the zeal for new learning come together. Our forebears warned us about this. For example, Baxter said, "Hard studies, much knowledge and excellent preaching are more glorious but still hypocritical sins when they are done for our glory."[13] Spurgeon also warned that pride grows as easily in the human heart as weeds on a dunghill.[14] This is true! Augustine said for those who want to live for the Lord, "This way is first humility, second humility, third humility."[15] And Calvin observed that "almost all corruptions of doctrine flow from the pride of men."[16]

---

[11] Wolfgang Metzger, "Die neōterikai epithymiai in 2 Timothy 2:22," *Theologische Zeitschrift* 33, no. 3 (1977): 129–136.

[12] I. Howard Marshall, *Pastoral Epistles*, ICC (London: T&T Clark, 1999), 764.

[13] Baxter, *The Reformed Pastor*, 13–14.

[14] "Consciousness of self-importance is a hateful delusion, but one into which we fall as naturally as weeds grow on a dunghill." In Charles Haddon Spurgeon, "Laid Aside. Why?" *Sword and the Trowel* (May 1876).

[15] Augustine, "Letter 118: To Dioscorus," in *Letters*, ed. Roy Joseph Deferrari, trans. Wilfrid Parsons, vol. 2:83–130, *Fathers of the Church* 18 (Washington, DC: The Catholic University of America Press, 1953), 282.

[16] John Calvin, *Commentary upon the Acts of the Apostles*, ed. Henry Beveridge, trans. Christopher Fetherstone, vol. 2 (Edinburgh: Calvin Translation Society, 1844), 258.

Alongside pride is the sin mentioned previously—which many believe is the direct referent of the command to flee youthful lusts—sexual sin. Several years ago, my brother (who is a pastor) and I were lamenting another friend in ministry who had an affair. As we thought about the situation and considered how to guard our own hearts, it dawned on us that all the men we knew who fell into sexual sin also exhibited the common factor of arrogance. The point is pride can not only lead you to pervert doctrine, it can lead you to pervert practice as well. But the opposite is true too. Humility will guard your soul or as John Owen said, "Some think they know enough already or perhaps they know all that is to be known of divine things. I expect no great discoveries of the mind of God from such persons."[17] Let us not be such persons.

Broadening our circle a bit to move our discussion forward, Josef Pieper says, "Those who look only at themselves do ever radiate nothing."[18] This observation is crucial because it shows holiness is not *all* that is needed to be a vessel the Lord can use. The dying world around us also needs us to radiate the life-giving truths of Christ, which you can only do if your focus is on him. So, a choice lies before you: focus on the Lord or focus on yourself. You must choose the Lord. When we do so, it should inspire us to pursue holiness not as those who have arrived, but as lead repenters who are aware of our sin, who flee to the cross, who are always aware of our need for grace and who serve as examples for people to follow. "Let others pretend they can attain to a sinless perfection. We dare not do it, but confess we are sinners."[19]

Finally, in verse 22, Paul says we must "pursue righteousness, faith, love and peace along with those who call on the Lord from

---

[17] John Owen, *Pneumatologia; Or A Discourse Concerning the Holy Spirit*, abridged by George Burder (Philadelphia, PA: Woodward, 1810), 333.

[18] Josef Pieper, *Only the Lover Sings: Art & Contemplation*, trans. Lothar Krauth (San Francisco, CA: Ignatius, 1990), 63. Pieper cites this saying as a Far Eastern proverb.

[19] Baxter, *The Reformed Pastor*, 9.

a pure heart." We see here that holiness is not something we strive for by ourselves. Sanctification is not an individual process. We do it with the church. This is why when believers say they will pursue holiness by themselves, I tell them they will fail. You cannot adequately train for future ministry in the church without being deeply involved in a specific local church during that time of preparation. To those who say they have not found just the *right* church in which to serve while in seminary, I would encourage you to start with a *wrong* one. Spurgeon said,

> If I had never joined a church until I had found one that was perfect—I would never have joined one at all. And the moment I did join it, if I had found one—I would have spoiled it, for it would not have been a perfect church after I had become a member of it. Still, imperfect as it is, it is the dearest place on earth to us.[20]

Just, get involved. I recall years ago when a student told me he had not found a good church because he already knew everything the churches in his area were teaching. I asked him how he could dare deprive a local church from such an amazing person as himself! Do not pretend to be serious about your seminary training unless you are committed to a specific local church. Pursue righteousness, faith and love *with* all those who call on the Lord out of a pure heart.[21]

3. A patient teacher (2 Timothy 2:24–26)

> [24] And the Lord's servant must not be quarrelsome but kind to everyone, able to teach, patiently enduring evil, [25] correcting

---

[20] Spurgeon, cited in Ron Rhodes, *1001 Unforgettable Quotes About God, Faith, & the Bible* (Eugene, OR: Harvest House, 2011), 38.

[21] Helmut Thielicke wisely said, "The church is our pastor." See *A Little Exercise for Young Theologians* (Grand Rapids, MI: Eerdmans, 1962), 26. This little booklet is a gold mine for anyone training for ministry.

his opponents with gentleness. God may perhaps grant them repentance leading to a knowledge of the truth, [26] and they may come to their senses and escape from the snare of the devil, after being captured by him to do his will.

Paul's last exhortation in this section is for Timothy (and any pastoral servant) to be a patient and gentle teacher, even with heretics. Why? Because God might grant them repentance. Always remember that one of the main reasons for your training is so you can lead people to eternal glory.[22] Your goal is not to win arguments. It is to lead people to their heavenly reward, and your efforts to that end are completely dependent on God's power to grant repentance. So speak, serve, love, help and plead for God to be at work in the hearts of people, especially those who may be going astray.

Likewise, this part of your calling always requires gentleness and compassion. Martin Bucer helpfully stated, "Those who wish to correct and win sinners according to Christ's command will by definition do this with a gentle spirit."[23] The language Paul uses here about those held captive or made captive by Satan is to elicit compassion. You are engaged in spiritual warfare. You will minister to people who are deceived by a fallen world under the dominion of the devil (1 John 5:19). People who are lost and away from the Lord may annoy you, but you must realize they are captives of Satan. They cannot free themselves from the chains that shackle them. That is why we speak the gospel—so God, by his life-giving Spirit, can cause the chains to fall off and people can go free. This is our task. This is the calling we have entrusted to us. It is large. It can be daunting.

---

[22] Baxter says "it is our duty to help others attain eternal glory." Cited in Thielicke, *A Little Exercise for Young Theologians*, 14.

[23] Martin Bucer, *Concerning the True Care of Souls*, trans. Peter Beale (Edinburgh, UK; Carlisle, PA: Banner of Truth, 2009), 102.

Conclusion

We must always be mindful the Lord is at work. The same gospel we share with a broken world is the same one sustaining us. If you find yourself questioning, "How can I be sufficient for these things?" keep in mind you are actually quoting Paul's own words from 2 Corinthians 2:16. You *are* insufficient on your own. You will be crushed serving in your own strength. But with God, he is able. He is willing. He is eager to bless his church through you.

While the calling to pastoral ministry is large and daunting, it is also glorious and God-empowered. This is why we must zealously pursue God's approval by devoting ourselves to understanding and living the Word of God. We must earnestly pursue holiness. We must grow into patient, loving teachers. The souls of men and women, boys and girls, are at stake. The glory of God among our community is at stake. Half-hearted measures will never do. May God give us all the grace to conform ourselves to this calling. The church is in need. The world is dying. Rise up to give your all for your King and find in his service fullness of life.

Shepherding a rebellious people
Exodus 32

Introduction
Read Exodus 32. This is quite a text: a missing leader, an anxious people, a golden calf, a raucous worship service and stern judgement, including the killing of many of the Israelites! There is much to learn in this text, but in this chapter I want to focus on what we see about leadership among the people of God. Moses is not a direct parallel of new covenant pastoral ministry, but there is enough overlap to give us some helpful lessons for those who would lead the people of God.

The people in Exodus 32 are pretty bad! And we *all* struggle with rebelling against God's ways. So, how should we respond when the people *we* are charged with leading turn away from God's commands? Aaron provides us with a negative example and Moses provides us with a positive example. Let's begin with the rebellious people.

A rebellious people

It was just in Exodus 20 that the Israelites received the Ten Commandments in which they were told, "Do not make graven images." Now, just twelve chapters later, they have made a graven image! As a result, the Lord himself says they have "turned aside quickly" (Exodus 32:8). Notice some aspects of their rebellion.

Grumbling

In the flow of the book of Exodus, we see they have been a grumbling people even before this incident (16:7–9, 12). The have complained about God. They have complained about food. God split the Red Sea, stacked it up on either side, walked them through and destroyed the world's superpower. And then they said, "Eh, the diet's not good." Really?!

"As a matter of fact, we wish we were in Egypt. Life was better before my redemption. Ever since I've lined up here with the Lord, it's been trouble! Back then I could enjoy a good sin. Now I can't even enjoy that."

Grumbling is a spiritual killer for all of us. That is why Paul exhorts,

> Do all things without grumbling or disputing, that you may be blameless and innocent, children of God without blemish in the midst of a crooked and twisted generation, among whom you shine as lights in the world (Philippians 2:14–15).

The Israelites were not shining here.

Impatience and a demanding spirit

Notice verse 1: "When the people saw that Moses delayed to come down from the mountain…." They are impatient. He delayed. Was it a delay in the Lord's timetable? Obviously not.

But they are only interested in their timetable. "What's he doing up there so long? Why doesn't he come now?"

Well, why should he come now? "Because we want him to come." Notice, even more, their language to Aaron: "Up, make us gods who shall go before us" (v. 1). A demanding spirit is clear here and is something the Lord always rebukes. There is even some discussion on the phrase "they gathered together to Aaron" (v. 1) suggesting that it shows hostility.[1] Aaron certainly claims such later—though he claims a lot of things. One way or the other, this was not a friendly gathering.

Dismissive

Now, hear the dismissiveness in their tone, "As for this Moses, the man who brought us up out of the land of Egypt, we do not know what has become of him" (v. 1). You get the idea. "He dragged us out here, and now we don't even know what became of him." That is a lack of faith. They know where he is, but he is not where they want him.

False worship/idolatry

They gave Aaron the gold, and when he made the calf, the people said, "These are your gods, O Israel, who brought you up out of the land of Egypt!" (v. 4). So, this calf is God. And notice at the end of verse five, Aaron says tomorrow shall be a feast "to the LORD." This is the personal name of God. These people, this rebellious people, are not choosing another religion. At least that's not what they are claiming. If we said to them, "You should worship only YHWH," they would say, "Of course! There he is! We're going to worship him."

We need to pay attention to the *form* of their idolatry, because whether we realize it or not, there are contemporary temptations along this line which may be more subtle than we realize. In the Ten Commandments the Lord did not just say do not worship

---

[1] See for example, Douglas K. Stuart, *Exodus*, vol. 2 (Nashville, TN: Broadman & Holman, 2006), 662.

any other God. He forbade making any images for worship. God forbade making any image of him which we would use for worship, thinking it is him.

The people are not claiming to worship Ra or Isis or any of the Egyptian gods. They want to worship Yhwh. They just want a visible form of him. All they're asking for is a culturally relevant form of worship. They still want to worship the Lord. They are not pagans. These are good people. They're earnest! They're demanding, "Give us our gods!" They don't cry out, "Give us our sins," but "Give us our gods!"

You can just hear them:

> I understand the Lord was invisible when he spoke, but we're just not used to invisible gods. That doesn't really cut it here in the Ancient Near East. I don't know if you understand my cultural situation. In my environment, in my culture, people don't do that. So, if you want to help engage me with your message, we need *visible* gods. Your invisible things—that's not gonna fly here. I don't know if you've done your demographic study or not. We need something visible. And as a matter of fact, we're kind of into calf gods. That's very common. We can get our minds around that. I mean, the Lord said he had a beef with it. He said it was a bunch of bull, but this is how we like to think about God.

I don't know if you've had conversations like this, but I have too often heard people say, "*I like to think about God like this. I like to think about God like that.*" Apart from being irrelevant, it is dangerous. God is self-defining. But they want this "culturally relevant," a little more user-friendly view of God. Not scary, not invisible, but visible and a calf. So they make it, and they have a feast. They're going to have worship, you see, because these are good church people. They're going to have a feast, just like you do in Israelite worship. They're going to have an altar, just like you do in Israelite worship.

Not only are they incorporating all sorts of things God has decreed, they also are hearty in their worship. When Moses and Joshua come down, Joshua can hear them. He thinks their singing is the sound of battle. What does that say about their singing? The text says they hear the shouts. This is robust engagement! They are excited! It also says they "rose up to play" (v. 6), which many suggest is a reference to sexual immorality.[2] This is how you worship the gods of Canaan. They are adapting biblical commands to common cultural expectations.

In response, Moses is angry. I can hear somebody today saying,

> Whoa, Moses, wait a minute, wait a minute. Cool off just a second. Why are you so upset? They've made an idol. Okay. But listen. Look at them for just a minute. This is a happening worship service. I mean, have you ever seen so much excitement among the people for worship? This certainly isn't sleepy or dull. I mean, this is how you reach the community. People are coming from all over for this and they can understand it. It's in the language they speak. We're doing the things they do. I know that immorality seems a little odd, but, hey, it's kind of in, and, and—wow—it sells!

They have the buzz, but they don't have God. It's not hard to stir up an event, to stir up excitement—and also stir up the wrath of God. These people have a happening worship service but they are about to die. We ought to consider that. When we think about worship discussions, there are a lot of nuances. I'm not saying this settles all the questions, but there are some weighty issues here and this is what they are doing: they have offended God.

God tells Moses: "Go down, for your people, whom you brought up out of the land of Egypt, have corrupted themselves" (v. 7). Parents, you know this tone. When one of your children

---

[2] For example, R. Alan Cole, *Exodus: An Introduction and Commentary* (Downers Grove, IL: InterVarsity Press, 1973), 226.

has disobeyed and you say to your spouse, "Do you know what your son did today?" Right? There's something like that here.

The Lord says his wrath burns hot against them (v. 10). They have corrupted themselves. The Lord says, "I have seen this people and behold it is a stiff-necked people" (v. 10). This is who these people are. Perhaps we have described them well enough to get the picture: this is a sinful people. So, let's move to the examples of leadership.

A bad example: Aaron

Appeasement

The bad example obviously is Aaron. First of all, they came to him in their sin, and they demanded an idol. Notice the way it says in verse 1, "the people gathered themselves together to Aaron." What do we have here? It's the majority. This is a Baptist people. They have had their business meeting; they have a majority vote and they expect to have their way. While I would affirm the role of the congregation, the majority does not necessarily indicate the will of God. They come in and demand of Aaron that he sin, and Aaron obeys. He's weak. He does not even put up any resistance. He just does what they tell him to do.

In verse 2 Aaron immediately follows, saying, "Okay, well, give me your gold." He receives the gold, fashions it with an engraving tool and makes a golden calf. That is important because when later he says "I threw it into the fire, and out came this calf" (v. 24), we already know that is not what happened. Rather, he *crafted* the idol they craved. Note the sense of intentionality here in this leader who knows the Word of God and yet caves to the pressure of the people. He, with his own hands, fashions the abomination to God and presents it to the people. And when they receive it, they say, "Yes, these are our gods!" You can almost hear Aaron say, "Boy, I'm glad they liked it. I'm glad they liked my abomination."

Notice the text says, "When Aaron saw this, he built an altar before it" (v. 5). When he saw the people were pleased with the idol, he took another step by providing a place for sacrifice to it. Furthermore, he made a proclamation, "Tomorrow shall be a feast to the LORD" (v. 5). Perhaps Aaron is seeking to excuse himself by tying the Lord in to this, trying to slip his appeasement of the people back into the approval of the Lord by calling this idol by the LORD's name. There is a temptation in leadership to acquiesce to the sinful desires of people and then slap the Lord's name on it and hope it will be acceptable. But it will not be acceptable to the One whose name in Holy.

Lack of discipline
If leaders appease the sinful desires of their people, then there will be no discipline. Note the observation in verse 25: "Moses saw that the people had broken loose (for Aaron had let them break loose, to the derision of their enemies)." Lack of discipline is weak leadership. Aaron had watched the people run off into sin and had said nothing. Their sinful behaviour had led to "the derision of their enemies."

What does that say about the church landscape around us? The Israelites changed their worship to be more like their neighbours, to be more understandable by their neighbors. You would think this would be more appealing to their neighbours. They began to act like their neighbours, but that did not result in great outreach. It just brought derision.

Do we not see this around us today? As often the church bends over backward to look like the world and to say, "Hey, we're not so bad. We look like you." The world stands back and says, "Hey, that's goofy. You look like us." Why should the world pay any attention to a church that already looks just like them? This is the opposite of the book of Acts, when there was a difference, and it says people feared to join them because they knew their God was real and was in their midst (Acts 5:13).

Where there is no discipline, there is no leadership, no pleasing of God, and thus no power. "When discipline leaves a church, Christ goes with it."[3]

Blame

We have seen Aaron's cowardly appeasement, but notice what else happens when Moses returns and confronts Aaron (vv. 21–24). Moses's anger and indignation are clear. Aaron's cringing shows up again as he says to Moses, "Let not the anger of my lord burn hot" (v. 22). He fears Moses's wrath but fails to understand that *God* is angered. We should be angered at what angers God. And we should fear the wrath of the LORD!

We observe the depth of Aaron's wickedness when he sells out the people, seeking to save himself by placing all the blame on them: "You know the people, that they are set on evil" (v. 22). "They made me do it, Moses. I know you've seen how bad they are with all they have put you through. Remember how wicked they were at the Red Sea? You know I wouldn't do something like this, but you know them. You can't trust them." This is a typical response of weak leaders. It goes back to the garden of Eden when God confronted Adam. Adam blamed Eve, Eve blamed the serpent and the serpent didn't have a leg to stand on.

Perhaps, men, you will recognize this. You may have been in a situation where there was a decision to be made, and you did not know what to do. Your wife had an opinion, so you went with that. Fine. But, then, when it bombed, you reminded her that it was *her* idea. That is textbook definition of weakness and passivity. This is what Aaron is doing. He made a decision, but now he wants to blame the people. People think someone is a good leader if he will do what they want. But that sort of leader will turn on you. Whatever the greatest power is he is confronted with, he will go with that. When the people are the great power, he will go with

---

[3] J.L. Dagg, *A Treatise on Church Order* (Charleston, SC: Southern Baptist Publication Society, 1858), 274.

them. But when a real leader shows up, he will flip and point his finger at them.

It is very easy for pastors to put the blame for the lack of health in our churches on the people. And pastors can comfort one another in this blame game. If you can blame your people, I can blame mine, and then we're all happy. And then we will go smile at them.

This is very tempting, particularly if you fall for a corporate business view of pastoral ministry. This view leads us to think that we need the church to succeed so that we, as CEOs, will look good. We can end up thinking of the church as a business to prosper rather than people to shepherd. Our pursuit of *success* can overwhelm actually *caring* for people. And when we think this way, the temptation comes to complain to God or to others: "If I had as good a church as that brother had, then I could be doing as good a work as he has. But I have difficult people. Why am I stuck here with difficult people?" All the while, of course, some of our people are saying, "If we had that pastor, we could be doing better. Why do we have to have this difficult guy?"

If a worldly view of success dominates our thinking, we are bound to complain. But Dietrich Bonhoeffer provides a helpful challenge to us at this point.

> A pastor should not complain about his congregation, certainly never to other people, but also not to God. A congregation has not been entrusted to him in order that he should become its accuser before God and men.[4]

God did not give us to our congregations that we might be their accusers. There is an accuser of the brethren (Revelation 12:10), but we are not to follow him. When we become our people's accuser, we have switched sides. Shall we conduct ourselves in such a way that in the end we hear our Master say, "You are of

---

[4] Dietrich Bonhoeffer, *Life Together* (New York: Harper Row, 1954), 29.

your father, the devil" (John 8:44) as he did to the Pharisees? This does not mean there is no place for rebuke or critique. We must do that, but there is a difference between correction and complaining. And we know it.

However, the desire to be impressive appears to be what is going on in this text. A desire to impress, a desire to have the crowd's favour, is a weakness. Now let's be clear here. We do desire the favour of God's people. We read that God blessed Joseph, giving him favour in the sight of people (Genesis 39:21). We do want the affection of our people. If you can pastor without desiring the affection of your people, something is wrong. However, you must not let that override everything else. And that is what is going on here. If we love people, we desire them to love us in return. But, we want—most of all—for them to love God.

Lying to cover our failure

Notice Aaron's claim that he just threw the gold in the fire and out popped this calf (v. 24)! Here is a common temptation: to stretch the truth to save our skins. It would be interesting to know what percentage of lies come about as attempts to rescue ourselves from our sins. Moses's confrontation is really a call to repentance, but Aaron turns to spin rather than confession, just like we too easily do when we fail to believe the gospel, which tells us that confession and repentance bring life. Too easily we think admitting to wrongdoing will bring destruction. But it is the lying attempt to avoid responsibility, to shift blame, to excuse ourselves, that brings destruction.

Our efforts to defend, excuse or explain away our sin are also quite often ludicrous and obviously false to others. Look again at Aaron's claim: "I threw it into the fire, and out came this calf" (v. 24). That's ridiculous! Unbridled grasping for self-preservation will drive you to say stupid things, to make a fool of yourself.

On the other hand, Aaron's statement might be a claim of divine intervention, a miracle. You can hear Aaron saying,

Hey, what was I to do? They came with this demand, and I wasn't real sure about it. You know how wicked they are. But they were pressing me, and I didn't know what to do. So I dropped the gold in the fire, and boom, look what happened. I mean, I didn't know if I was supposed to do that, but then all these circumstances lined up. Surely that meant it was God's will.

If this was a claim for a miracle, then notice whom Aaron is blaming: God!

"You know, I didn't want to, to cheat on this test. But then that paper was right there, and I could see it." "I didn't want to hide this part of my income, but then there was this opportunity, and I did it." "I didn't want to gossip, but then the person asked that question just the right way." There are all kinds of ways of blaming God. We are very good at excusing ourselves and blaming God for our errors. The most common one is simply to claim you "felt led" to do something. Some people think a subjective impression of God's leading trumps any other concerns. I do not doubt there is a subjective element to the Lord's leading, but it never violates the objective truth of God's Word. Whatever is going on with Aaron here, he is blaming the people, blaming God and excusing himself.

You can imagine a contemporary parallel. "Pastor, make us an idol. If you don't, we'll fire you." There are a lot of Aarons out there who will make you whatever calf you want. Some congregations will even say, "If you won't make us the idol we want, we'll fire you and get another pastor. We have resumés right here that say this guy will make idols for us." I've seen some of those resumés. Part of what it looks like to shepherd rebellious people is not to give in to their sinful demands. Shepherding rebellious people means standing on the truth of God's Word and saying, "No," when it is necessary to say no. "No, because I love you too much to lead you into sin, to be a part of your rebellion. I'd rather you reject me than to help you in rejecting God."

Someone might object, "But I might get fired." The real answer to that is, "Welcome to the suffering of the people of God which has occurred across the ages." I do not say that lightly. There is a way to talk with swagger in such discussions, but this is real. It costs. It really hurts. But that is what the people of God have done through the ages. There are numerous historical examples. I think of the Rescissory Act (1661) in Scotland, when hundreds of pastors who refused to bow to the government were ejected from their churches. Hundreds of Scottish pastors refused to violate their conscience and, along with their wives, took their children in their arms and trudged out into a Scottish winter because they would not bow.[5] We have a heritage. Let us live up to it. We must not acquiesce to the sinful demands of any people. We should pray with Luther, "Grant us unflinching faith to abide in your Word that we yield not one jot or tittle of your truth to please men."[6]

Notice what Moses says in verse 21: "What did this people do to you that you have brought such a great sin upon them?" That's a powerful statement. It is not what I was expecting. I was expecting something like, "Why did you do this?" But Moses's question includes an assumption that gives Aaron more credit than he deserves. The question assumes they must have done something to Aaron to cause him to do such evil.

> Brother, good gracious. Oh, what must have happened to you? I'm worried about you that you've done this, but, but your eyes are both still there. Both ears are attached. There are no bruises or welts. Where is the skin hanging from your back for surely, they beat you to within an inch of your life for you to have done such a thing.

---

[5] See K.M. Brown, "Covenanters," in *Dictionary of Scottish Church History and Theology*, ed. Nigel M. de S. Cameron (Downers Grove, IL: InterVarsity Press, 1993), 219; J.M. Dryerre, *Heroes and Heroines of the Scottish Covenanters* (Edinburgh: The Religious Book and Tract Society, 1907), 17.

[6] *Reading the Psalms with Luther*, trans. Bruce Cameron (St. Louis, MO: Concordia Publishing House, 2007), 199.

In fact, all they had to do was posture, make a little threatening move. It did not take much for Aaron to cave. How about you?

When I look at Aaron's capitulation, I think of my limited exposure to brothers and sisters in other places. A few years ago, I was in Nepal and gathered with a church for worship. The people were packed in and, in the middle of the service as more people came in, the deacons nudged us over to make more room. There were no chairs. People were just seated on the floor. As we watched people coming in, a translator sitting next to me in the back told me stories about the different people. He pointed out one of the elders and told me he had been a Buddhist priest. When he came to faith, a mob came and burned his house to the ground. They beat him and hung him up by his feet, leaving him there for a couple of days. And now here he was preaching the gospel of Jesus Christ. As the man was telling me this story, I was watching the elder worshipping the Lord. He was not complaining about what he had endured. He was just worshipping the Lord, rejoicing that he had come to know the one true God.

Then a man came in quite late, staggering a bit. He did not look quite right. One side of his face was sunk in. I thought he was probably a homeless man wandering in drunk. I wondered what the people would do. I wondered if this would be a little embarrassing. Then my translator pointed out the man and asked if I wanted to know his story? Sure! That man was part of the first generation of believers in Nepal. During that time, persecution was even worse and he was arrested and beaten. My translator said, "You may notice his face looks a little different. That is because when they beat him, they broke all the bones on this side of his face." They did not have the medical care we take for granted here. There was no reconstructive surgery, so his face remained sunken in. He was one of their heroes of the faith. And there he was worshipping the Lord with no complaint.

The leader of the church we were visiting, which was planting dozens of others in the area, had been in prison multiple times, had lines between his fingers where they took blades and sliced it and poured in peppers and sauce to torment him. Stories like these flood into my mind as I hear Moses saying to Aaron, "What did these people do to you that you agreed to follow them in their sin?" What have your people done to you to cause you to avoid obedience?

When people we shepherd move toward rebellion, we must be willing to stand fast on God's Word, regardless of the cost. Pastor, love them too much to bring "such a great sin upon them" (v. 21). Do not shift the blame or lie or blame God to cover yourself.

A good example: Moses
Now let's look at the example of faithful leadership in Moses.

Care and intercession
Look back to verse 7, where the Lord speaks to Moses and gives him his rebuke of the people. The Lord gives him an option, which sounds like an amazing one. How could it be refused? The Lord says,

> I have seen this people, and behold, it is a stiff-necked people Now therefore let me alone, that my wrath may burn hot against them and I may consume them, in order that I may make a great nation of you (vv. 9–10).

We might find ourselves reading this text saying, "Lord I'm ready! Destroy my people and make a great nation for me. I'm ready!" Moses has the opportunity not only to be the lawgiver, but to be the father of the people (like Abraham). This is an offer for a great promotion. This is not even Moses's complaining to God, and God's saying, "Okay, I will move you." This is God's offering: "I'll wipe them out. They are sinful. They deserve it." The language is interesting though. God, the Almighty, says to Moses, a human, "Leave me alone and I will do this. Step back and don't stop me. Then I will do this." What power does Moses have to stop the Lord? I think the Lord here is teaching Moses. I think

God is stirring up Moses, essentially asking, "What will you do, Moses? What will be your heart?" And Moses gives the proper response. He has the offer for an advancement, to be more humanly speaking than he has been before, to get rid of people who have been a pain to him. He has been annoyed with them. They are very rebellious. And yet his first response is, "O LORD, why does your wrath burn hot against your people?" We may think, "What?! Do you have to ask that question?" But Moses refers to the people as those "whom you have brought out." Remember the Lord referred to them as the ones Moses brought out (v. 7). Moses says, "No Lord, you brought them out with great power and a mighty hand." Instead of Moses's being the accuser of the brethren, he becomes their intercessor. Do the people deserve destruction? You better believe it. But Moses says, "Oh God, forgive your people."

Notice he has two grounds for intercession. First, he pleads on the basis of *the glory of God*: "Why should the Egyptians say, 'With evil intent did he bring them out, to kill them in the mountains and to consume them from the face of the earth'?" (v. 12). In other words,

> Lord, you have rescued your people. You have brought them out. You have embarrassed the gods of Egypt. Everyone in Egypt knows the God of Israel is a true God. Everyone knows the God of Israel has trumped the gods of Egypt. They stand in wonder, and they are watching. What will they say of you if you consume them here? "Well, sure that god can beat us, but you don't want to serve him. He'll destroy you."

He is arguing not on the goodness of the people, but on the reputation of God. We need to be those pastors who intercede for our people in the depth of their sin and on the basis of the reputation of God.

The second ground for Moses's intercession is *the covenant*:

> Remember Abraham, Isaac, and Israel, your servants, to whom you swore by your own self, and said to them, "I will multiply your offspring as the stars of heaven, and all this land that I have promised I will give to your offspring, and they shall inherit it forever" (v. 13).

Someone could say God would still accomplish the covenantal promise by making a nation out of Moses. The line would still be preserved. But, Moses pleads essentially, "Lord, you promised to bless and to increase these people, not to destroy them."

Moses pleads on the basis of the glory of God and the promises of God. We need to be pastors who pray with concern for God's reputation while reminding him of his promises. Not because God forgets, but that we say to the Lord, "I know you have said this is what you intend to do. So, I will stand on that." Let us pray in this way because then we ask in confidence.

In response to such prayer, it says "the Lord relented from the disaster that he had spoken of bringing on his people" (v. 14). The Lord does not change his mind as a man does (Numbers 23:19). But the Lord was drawing out the heart of Moses, the true leader, just as he did when he came to the garden after Adam and Eve had eaten and asked them, "Where are you?" It is not that the Lord could not find them. Rather, it is like when I would find my two-year-old with his blanket over his head and cookie crumbs all around when he was not supposed to get a cookie. He thought I could not see him. I would ask, "Benjamin, where are you?" I was not asking for information. I was inviting him to repentance. So here, the Lord's offer is an invitation for the pastor's heart to rise up.

Maybe you are in a very difficult situation right now. Maybe there are people mounted against you. Maybe the Lord has you there to train and draw out in you a pastor's heart that will intercede for his people. Some people may show themselves not to be true believers. We will see that in a moment in this text. But in the meantime, we intercede.

Mercy

Such care and intercession arise from mercy and here Moses reflects the character of God. Where does such mercy in a person come from? The text does not speak to this, but my mind turns to Exodus 4, that odd text where the LORD comes to kill Moses because he has not had his son circumcised. It is a challenging text, often not dealt with significantly in commentaries. A key point in the text is that Moses is reminded that the requirements of the law apply to him as much as anyone else. Because he failed to obey the law, he was worthy of death. Yet, when Zipporah circumcised the child, in essence repenting, God relented. Moses had a brush with the judgement he deserved but found mercy.

Those who have known their deep need of mercy are the most prepared to extend mercy to others, for it is those who have been forgiven much who love much (Luke 7:47). As William Gurnall wrote, "None will handle poor souls so gently as those who remember the smart of their own heart-sorrows."[7] The truth is: if we have been saved, we *all* have been forgiven much. Even if you were saved as a child and never had a "rebellious stage," you have been forgiven much because any sin deserves hell. If we do not realize we have been forgiven much, we will be self-righteous damnation-mongers rather than ministers of the gospel of the grace of God. We will not be ready to intercede for our people unless we are deeply aware of our own sin and need for mercy.

Confrontation

Moses intercedes. He pleads for the people. In human terms, he secures their preservation. Only then does he go down the mountain and confront the people. We have seen his care for the people, his plea for mercy, so we might think he will go easy on their sin. But nothing could be further from the truth. Good leadership

---

[7] William Gurnall, *The Christian in Complete Armour* (Peabody, MA: Hendrickson, 2010), 105.

must confront sin with rebuke, a call to repentance and restoration or removal. This is the opposite of appeasement.

Moses arrives with *rebuke*. His anger burns against the people. He throws the tablets of the Ten Commandments to the ground. He takes the calf, burns it, grinds it to powder, throws it in the water and compels the people to drink it! This may confuse readers if we fail to see that mercy and accountability go together. He has asked God not to destroy the people, but this does not mean sin will be excused. He has asked for them to have an opportunity to repent. But they will be disciplined, and then there will be an opportunity for repentance. Those who repent will be restored. Those who do not will be destroyed. Only the person who knows he deserves death and understands mercy is prepared to lead in discipline. Discipline will be firm in places, but it will come through one who has pleaded with God, with tears, for the people. That heart will shape even the judgement. So now judgement has to come.

When confronted with rebellion against God's ways, a leader must rebuke sin. It must be clear and firm. It must not be confused with personal agendas (we have already seen Moses reject the lure of personal agenda). This means a leader must point out deviation from God's Word in direct terms and say precisely what God says about the sin. Moses's anger burns because God's anger burns.

Then we see the call to *repentance*, as Moses cries out, "Who is on the Lord's side? Come to me" (v. 26). No matter what has happened up until this point, there is a call for any who will to come to the "Lord's side." Leading in the midst of rebellion must involve calling people to repentance. It is not enough to decry sin. We must point out the way of rescue in repentance. "Return to the Lord!" These people have been involved in deep sin, but still the offer of repentance is there. This is the glory of the gospel for sinful people like us. If we will indeed confess our sins, own the fact that our behaviour is wrong and offensive to God, take responsibility for our behaviour, then "he is faithful and just to forgive us our sins and to cleanse us from all unrighteousness" (1 John 1:9).

Once there is rebuke and call to repentance, then those who respond are restored and those who do not respond are removed. In Exodus 3:2 those who do not turn to the Lord are executed, about 3,000 men. How does this apply today? The New Testament parallel to being "cut off from the people" is excommunication, where people are removed from the community. If people will not repent but continue in their rebellion, then they must be excommunicated (see Matthew 18:15–20; 1 Corinthians 5), and shepherds must lead in this process. This is a difficult, painful task, but there is no way to be faithful while avoiding this task.

What then does it look like to shepherd a rebellious people? Unlike Aaron, it means to say no to selfish desires. It means to intercede for people and not give up on them. It means to call people to repentance. It means, when necessary, to take the steps of discipline, so the Lord would be pleased. "Conflict is inevitable unless men passively yield to the power of evil."[8]

We see even more intercession at the end of the chapter. Moses says to the Lord, "But now, if you will forgive their sin—but if not, please blot me out of your book that you have written" (v. 32). That is powerful! It is no mere lofty rhetoric. Paul echoes this sentiment in the New Testament, saying he would, if it were possible, desire for himself to be condemned if it would secure the salvation of his countrymen (see Romans 9:1–5).

I marvel at Moses' statement. *Would I be willing to say this directly to God?* This is a man who cares deeply for his people. This is the kind of prayer that guards souls. Even later, when the Lord says he will allow the people to go on to the Promised Land but he will not go with them, Moses will not relent. He hangs on to the Lord until the Lord says he will not destroy them. And he hangs on longer until the Lord says he will forgive them. He will hang on longer until God says, "My presence will go with you"

---

[8] B.F. Westcott, *The Epistles of St John* (London: Macmillan and Co, 1883), 60.

(see Exodus 33). That is what we need to be doing as we shepherd the people of God—persevering prayer for the preservation of the people.

Conclusion

We have considered lessons for pastors as we lead God's people. But, as I noted at the start of the chapter, Moses is not primarily a *type* of pastor. We cannot live up to all that we see here. We have seen the sinfulness of the people of God. The law was just given, and they could not obey it. We have not obeyed either. We see that from the very beginning, the old covenant was broken. We see even then the need for the new covenant. We see that the covenant of Moses will not suffice. We need the covenant of Christ. We need one not simply who will be a human among us, but who will be God come to earth in human form, who will lead us and who will intercede for us as the great High Priest, and who will atone for our sins and ascend to the presence of God. And so, Jesus Christ emerges here. It really is *his* portrait. He is the great Shepherd of the sheep whom we follow as the under-shepherds of his sheep.

It makes sense, then to close this chapter with a prayer to the God and Father of our Lord Jesus Christ:

> Father, thank you that you are a persevering God, and you have had mercy on our souls. Forgive us, Lord, where we have been judgemental, where we have been mindful of the sins of others but not of ourselves. Forgive us, on the other hand, Lord, where we have been sinfully indulgent in the sins of our people and have failed to love them enough to risk ourselves and rebuke them. Lord, we are torn and we again are feeble and frail. It is so easy to err on the side of indulgence, or then to feel bad for that and swing to the other side and err on the side of wrongful severity. Put the whole together. Mercy and discipline together are a challenge for us. And yet you call us to it. So we ask you, guide us great

Jehovah. Empower us that we might do your will so your church would be strengthened, your people would be edified, we would love, defend and care for your people as you deserve, so our enemies would not deride you, but your glory would be seen and your kingdom would advance. In Jesus' name. Amen.

Brothers, hold fast![1]

Introduction

I heard someone recently say, "If this ain't difficult times, they'll do until difficult times come!"[2] Some of you may feel like the guy in the P.G. Wodehouse novel described as "A melancholy-looking man, he had the appearance of one who has searched for the leak in life's gas-pipe with a lighted candle."[3]

The fact is pastoring is challenging work. Too often it is thankless. And pastors' wives often feel it even more deeply than we do. Slights against the one you love are often harder to forgive than slights against yourself.

---

[1] This chapter is adapted from a talk that was originally given at a Pastors' Appreciation Banquet at Union University in 2020.

[2] Mike Holley, "7 simple suggestions for leading in a crisis," n. 17, https://www.tdcaa.com/journal/%ef%bb%bf7-simple-suggestions-for-leading-in-a-crisis/.

[3] P.G. Wodehouse, "The Man Who Disliked Cats," in *The Man Upstairs and Other Stories* (London: Barrie and Jenkins, 1971), 92.

People can insult you when they are not even trying to! Comments after sermons are some of the easy examples. Early in my ministry, after I had preached one Sunday, a dear lady said to me, "You're going to be a good little preacher one day." I knew she meant well, so it just struck me as humorous. It held out hope that one day I'd do well. Apparently not *today*, but one day. However, the hope is limited since what I will one day attain to is being a good *little* preacher. I'm not sure exactly what that would be, but I am pretty sure that is not what I had aspired to. We all have our stories when people have zinged us, even when they meant to be encouraging.

Then there was Mrs. Maudie, an elderly lady in a church I pastored in Wisconsin. I was including more Scripture reading in our worship services and one Sunday as she left after the service, Mrs. Maudie, in her gruff way said, "If you'd read one more verse this morning I was going to walk out!" I just smiled and said, "Why, Mrs. Maudie, if I'd known that I'd have read one more." She actually appreciated that sort of give and take.

But, too many people in our churches are not just gruff or stumbling over intended compliments. Some are difficult and simply mean. As one pastor said to me, "People aren't at their best right now, and some seem to think they can take it out on pastors because they think we have to be nice." This sort of tension can just weigh on you, eating away at your soul, even some times causing you to take more offense at things than you normally would.

Samuel Rutherford, the great Scottish preacher, is a wonderful companion in trying times. To friends and church members he wrote, "You are in the common way to heaven when you are under our Lord's crosses," and "I know that an afflicted life looks very like the way that leads to the kingdom" (Acts 15:22).[4]

---

[4] Samuel Rutherford, *Letters of Samuel Rutherford*, ed. A.A. Bonar (Edinburgh: Oliphant, Anderson & Ferrier, 1891) 58, 50.

Rutherford went on to say to one in the midst of suffering, "Count much of your Master's smiling."[5] Of course, the problem is, when you are down, you do not think he is smiling at you. Let me remind you that when you continue to labour faithfully, simply plodding along though no one notices, the Lord smiles upon you. When you work hard at your sermon preparation, even though when it comes time to deliver it seems to fail, when you labour for the best way to arrange services in light of obstacles, still he smiles. You know this, but I need you to hear it from someone outside your own head: God's love for you is not dependent on others evaluation of you. His love for you does not wax and wane with the opinion of your church. Your God is for you. He is with you, and he is steady. So hold fast.

Hear Rutherford's words to a faithful sufferer once again: "My Master bade me tell you, God's blessing shall be upon you for it."[6] And so I am here on behalf of the Master to say to you, as you faithfully serve the Lord, regardless of whatever else is going on around you, his blessings are on you for it.

Central to our perseverance and joy in difficult times is the *hope of the resurrection*. After his powerful exposition of the resurrection in 1 Corinthians 15, Paul concludes with this exhortation, which we need to take to heart:

> Therefore, my beloved brothers, be steadfast, immovable, always abounding in the work of the Lord, knowing that in the Lord your labor is not in vain (1 Corinthians 15:58).

Let me point out three basic points from this text.

1. Be steadfast, immovable
Do not doubt in the dark what you knew in the light. You know the truth of God. You know who he is. You know his Word is true.

---

[5] Rutherford, *Letters*, 54.
[6] Rutherford, *Letters*, 55.

When things are difficult and you hurt or are confused or uncertain, hold on to what you knew was true in the light. "Be steadfast, immovable." That does not mean you hold fast to your own opinions and no one can persuade you to see something differently, but you hold to God's Word.

All around us, people are being swept away. People are giving in. People are changing their opinions about God, about his Word, about the teachings of his Word. They seem to be chasing cultural acceptance rather than the favour of God. Be steadfast; be immovable. We see leaders fail and compromise. And too often, somebody will say to me, "Well, do you still believe that?" "Yes." "But didn't you know that this big name has changed his opinion?" My answer is, "Who is he to me? God's Word has not changed." I am grieved when I see people move away from the Scriptures, but I am not moved. The right side of history will be revealed at the judgement seat of Christ.

As people compromise and let us down, we must remember,

> My hope is built on nothing less
>   than Jesus' blood and righteousness.
> I dare not trust the sweetest frame, [or some leaders' fame]
>   but wholly lean on Jesus' name.
> On Christ, the solid rock, we stand.
>   All other ground is sinking sand.

It really does not matter who turns another way. God has spoken. What he said 2,000 years ago was true 1,000 years later and is true today. He has shown himself true in so many ways, chiefly or ultimately in the resurrection. So brothers, "Be steadfast, immovable."

2. Be always abounding in the work of the Lord

Don't stop. Keep going.

Keep on abounding. You might say, "I don't feel like I'm abounding right now. I don't know if I can keep on abounding."

Stay at it. Stay at this steady, faithful work. One of the real problems that affects us in church ministry today is this idea that the grand, the spectacular, the big splash is what demonstrates God's favour. But look through the Scriptures, and you will see this is not so. Brothers, keep plodding. When you are working on your sermon and the last one felt like it fell apart and this one just does not seem like it is going to come together, keep plodding. When you are not even sure who is going to be hearing it anyway, whether there will be many people there, keep plodding.

Even as you read this there might be some souls who are bruised reeds. Maybe some of you are thinking, "That's not me. I haven't been doing that." Maybe even my words, which are meant to encourage, might feel like discouragement. "I'm not doing what I need to do. I've not done all that I need to do." Remember Peter, after his failure. When Jesus came to him to restore him, he didn't ask, "How hard will you work?" He didn't ask, "How smart are you?" He didn't ask, "How important are you?" He just asked, "Do you love me?" Do *you* love Jesus? I know you do. And he is ready to restore us and continue to use us.

Do not worry, then, about the standards of importance or success. Just love him, hold fast to him and then serve and love his people. He will be pleased, and, in that, you can be pleased. He called us knowing we were as messed up as we are. He knew more of our sin than we knew at the time. But he brings us back to the cross. He will restore. He will continue to use. And let me just stress here too that though it is a sin to give up on the Lord, it is not a sin to be discouraged.

Here is another familiar text. Jesus at Gethsemane says to the disciples with him, "My soul is deeply grieved to the point of death" (Matthew 26:38, NASB). This is the sinless Saviour speaking. You may face some times when you are deeply grieved on the pathway to the kingdom. Remember, our Lord and Master was there. It is no shame if you find yourself there. But remember what he said in that situation, when he asked, "My Father, if it be possible, let this cup pass from me." But then he said,

"Nevertheless, not as I will, but as you will" (Matthew 26:39, ESV). It is another way of saying, "Keep on abounding. Keep plodding." He calls us to be steadfast, immovable. He calls us to keep abounding, to keep plodding.

If 1 Corinthians 15:58 ended with "Be steadfast, immovable, always abounding in the work of the Lord" that would be a pretty rough story because it would basically be, "Pull yourself up by your bootstraps." That works okay until you do it enough, then you break your bootstraps—and there is just not enough in us to get it done. So that is not where Paul ends. The last part of the verse points us to the *hope* that empowers this perseverance.

3. Know that in the Lord your labour is not in vain

The *resurrection* is the ground of our hope. Paul reminds us our labour—whatever it is, whatever it feels like right now, whatever the response is right now—because there is a resurrection, is not in vain. God will not allow one drop of your sweat or blood to drop in vain.

Right now you may feel overwhelmed with the sense that you have poured out your heart and absolutely nothing is coming from it, but we must remember not to trust in our feelings. If I can borrow Rutherford's language, "My Master bade me tell you, your labour is not in vain." On the authority of God's Word, as you faithfully serve him, your labour is not in vain. Of course, we want to see the results. I love it when I can see the results of God at work through me, and that is good and fine. The Lord sometimes blesses us by letting us see a result, a life changed. But we are not promised that. I think sometimes, in my own life, God does not let me see or even feel the results. I think sometimes the Lord withholds that just to remind me, "I'm the one doing this, not you."

Whether or not you can see what God is doing, your labour in him is not in vain. Your faithful, steady service is accomplishing more than you can see, more than you can know. This is seen throughout Scripture and has become one of my favourite truths. Recall Haggai 1 where Haggai is preaching, "Rebuild the temple."

When the people obey, we are surprised because they had not been very obedient by this time in the Old Testament. The temple is rebuilt—this is amazing! And the younger people celebrate. You can hear the celebration a long way off. But the older people mourn and weep because this new temple was so small and unimpressive. They remembered Solomon's temple. You can imagine the people saying, "*This* is the new temple? Are you kidding me? This is what Haggai was sent by God to tell us to do? It might have been better to do nothing rather than to do this. It's an embarrassment. God can't be pleased with this. This doesn't show the glory of God."

But God, through the prophet, says, "The latter glory of this house shall be greater than the former" (Haggai 2:9). Now, if I were there, I would be scratching my head and thinking, *I don't see it. I mean, you can do a big-time makeover on this little thing and it is still not going to be more glorious than Solomon's temple.* I think the people who heard that prophecy probably died wondering how this would *ever* be. But you and I know it was.

As we read along in the Scriptures, Herod comes along. He does some refurbishing, but it is still not like Solomon's temple. However, it is at that "little" temple where the Lord Jesus is presented as a child. It is that little temple where Jesus comes teaching and preaching. It is that little temple where the veil is torn in two[7] when Jesus inaugurates the new and living way into the presence of the Lord.[8] That little temple—its glory was far greater than the earlier temple because of *who* came there and what he did. But the people who built it did not see that at the time. God was doing more than they could imagine.

Right now, as you labour, there are times you may be tempted to think, "This is nothing." Some people may say to you, "This is nothing. You're telling us to do these things but it looks pretty sad." Remember, God is doing more than you could ever imagine.

---

[7] Matthew 27:51.
[8] Hebrews 10:20.

Consider the Lord Jesus at Gethsemane. With merely human eyes, what do we see? We see a travelling teacher who has gotten a lot of attention and now he is in trouble. His "soul is very sorrowful, even to death" (Matthew 26:38). He is about to be killed. Humanly speaking, his situation is very dire. But in that moment, God is at work "reconciling the world to himself" (2 Corinthians 5:19). God is there—in that moment which looks like complete defeat—rescuing my soul and yours. God is doing *more* than you can imagine. This reality is the basis for Paul's reminder: "…knowing that *in the Lord* your labor is not in vain" (1 Corinthians 15:58).

Pastors, we are going to see this in the resurrection. We are going to have to die in hope because we are not going to see it all revealed in our lifetime. Some of you may see more results than others, and we should thank God when we see it. But what we are waiting on is the final day—that is when we will see all that God has accomplished through our labours.

In 2009, my older brother died in a freak accident. Totally out of the blue, I got a call just after I had barely fallen asleep. It was rough. I went to be with my family, and after the funeral I came home for a conference I was supposed to lead. As I was moving about attending to last minute things as attendees were arriving, a man who meant well caught me and asked how I was doing. I thanked him and told him I was doing ok. It was not the time but apparently he thought I was not facing the heartache of the situation enough (even though he did not know me very well). So he began, "Pain. Pain. Pain that will last forever." You know, some people just have the gift of encouragement. I thought, "Why are you saying this to me? I assume you think you're trying to help me face the reality of something. This is not helpful." But without me thinking about it, something just welled up inside of me. I did not say this aloud, but there welled up inside of me a deep *No!* Pain, yes. Deep pain, yes. But that will not last forever. There is a resurrection. There is a great, getting-up Sunday, when all will be made right, the dead in Christ will rise, his truth will be vindicated and God himself will wipe away all our tears. So, yes, pain. Yes, it is not all great right now, but there is coming a day when that will be gone. Pain is real now, but it does not have the last word. And on *that* day, we will be able to see what God has been up to!

We cannot see it now. This is why "we walk by faith, not by sight" (2 Corinthians 5:7). We live in hope. You may say, "But I *want* to see." I know. I do too. But he calls us to trust him. He calls us to rest in him.

When our children were young, I often would take my boys on little hikes near our house. I would typically make up a story about what adventure we were on as we walked. One year, around Christmas, we crossed the road into a field as knights on a grand adventure, waylaying the bad guys with our sticks as swords. Along the way, we came upon a manhole right next to a train track. I was spinning a tale, so of course there was a princess down there and we rescued her (without going down the manhole—this is pretend, remember!). And then I began to realize, "Wait a minute, we've got to get back. We're about to be late for an event!" I did not want to abandon the story and the fun, so I had to create a turn in the story. I addressed the three young boys before me, aged between five and two: "Men, we've got a decision to make. We've got the princess here. We're going to put her on this train. We can jump the train with her and go. In that case we will be safe, but she may be in danger. But if we want to ensure her safety, we'll put her on the train and we'll turn and fight. If we do that, I can promise you, we will slow down the bad guys long enough that she'll be safe. But, men, I can't promise you that we'll make it. So what's the choice?" They raised their sticks and yelled, "We fight, daddy!" Yes! So we destroyed much grass and tall weeds as we made our way back home, marching quickly, as I got increasingly worried about making us late to this event.

As we pressed on, I ended up having to carry my youngest son. As I pressed us on faster and worried more about the time, the story faded from my mind. I was simply trudging along, while carrying one child and watching another who was trailing behind. Then, out of the quiet, my second son walking beside me said matter-of-factly, "Daddy, I don't think I'm going to make it." I realized all of a sudden he was still "in character" in the story. So, I said, "Why is that, buddy?" Huffing and puffing, he said, "Well, I just don't think I'm going to make it. But if I don't make it, the worst thing is I won't get to see Mama and baby again." Then he said, "But, Daddy, if I don't make it, you tell Mama it's okay because I'll see her again in heaven one day."

That struck my heart. Perseverance empowered by hope of the resurrection. I prayed silently, *Oh God, my boy is only playing, but he's handling great gospel truth right here. Would you please take that truth deep into his heart so that when he is grown, he might also be willing to say it's worth it to lay it all on the line, to spend and be spent for the gospel because it will be okay because there is a resurrection?* I want to urge you, brothers, in light of the resurrection, it is worth it to lay it all on the line for the Lord. He sees you.

Conclusion

The Lord will vindicate your faithful labours. Take heart, brothers, your labour is not in vain. The Lord is with you. To quote Rutherford once again, "Patience, my beloved; Christ the King is coming home."[9] May you be

> strengthened with all power, according to his glorious might, for all endurance and patience with joy; giving thanks to the Father, who has qualified you to share in the inheritance of the saints in light (Colossians 1:11–12).

---

[9] Rutherford, *Letters*, 54.

Discover other titles from Heritage Seminary Press

A "phoenix of women": Puritan spirituality in the letters of Brilliana Harley
Introduced and edited by Michael A.G. Azad Haykin

The life of Lady Brilliana Harley was marked by a deep and living relationship with God. A Puritan Presbyterian by conviction, Brilliana was shunned by her neighbours during the tumultuous English Civil Wars and is remembered as valiantly resisting the siege of her home by the forces of Charles I.

Brilliana's letters reveal the heart of her spirituality. While concerned about her son Edward (Ned)'s studies at Oxford, his diet and exercise, she especially encourages him about the value of a vital relationship with God. Her letters also expose the breadth of her reading and her theological acumen. As the troubles around her increased, she took increasing solace in the truths of election, the sufficiency of Christ's work and the sovereignty of God. The soil of her heart was truly warmed by "the sweet waters of God's Word."

ISBN 978-1-77484-152-5 (Pbk)
ISBN 978-1-77484-153-2 (Ebook)
172 pages; 5.5 x 8.5"
Published September 2024

An imprint of H&E Publishing
hesedandemet.com

Discover other titles from Heritage Seminary Press

Life is Worship: A *festschrift* in honour of Douglas A. Thomson
Editors: David G. Barker & Michael A.G. Haykin

These essays honour the life and ministry of Dr. Doug Thomson who, as a teacher, pastor, colleague and music leader, has influenced countless lives and congregations in Ontario, Canada, and beyond. The themes of these chapters cover areas that are precious in the life of the church—revealing how all of life is worship.

Topics include expositions of psalms and hymns, the theology of worship, spirituals, hallmarks of a worship leader, friendship in the composition of hymns, lament, etc.—even some sermons for Easter weekend. It is hoped that these essays will encourage discussion, promote the development of an understanding of the theology around worship, challenge readers to think deeply about this crucial area and, most of all, bring glory and praise to our great God.

ISBN 978-1-77484-128-0 (Pbk)
ISBN 978-1-77484-129-7 (Ebook)
364 pages; 6 x 9"
Published September 2023

An imprint of H&E Publishing
hesedandemet.com

Discover other titles from Heritage Seminary Press

This Poor Man Called: Stories and Songs of David
Volume 1 & Volume 2
By **David G. Barker**

David Barker takes a unique approach in this exploration of the psalms of David. Each chapter begins with a creative retelling of the biblical narrative, setting the scene for the psalm arising out of that experience. Having grounded the psalm in the "story," Barker then goes into a verse-by-verse exposition of the psalm, and provides some explanatory notes and a statement of the key message of the psalm.

At the end of each psalm exposition, Barker asks three basic questions: What do we learn about God? What do we learn about ourselves as the people of God? and What do we learn about the world? Answering these questions helps us to understand how David's experience shaped his theocentric and biblical worldview.

Volume 1
ISBN 978-1-77484-063-4 (Pbk)
ISBN 978-1-77484-064-1 (Ebook)
122 pages; 5.5 x 8.5"
Published Spring 2022

Volume 2
ISBN 978-1-77484-110-5 (Pbk)
ISBN 978-1-77484-111-2 (Ebook)
192 pages; 5.5 x 8.5"
Published February 2023

An imprint of H&E Publishing
hesedandemet.com

Discover other titles from Heritage Seminary Press

Losing Your Luggage: Finding Freedom from Sinful Baggage
By Rick Reed

Losing Your Luggage takes you on a journey through Romans 6–8, helping you find freedom from the sinful baggage that weighs you down. Your guide for this trip is Rick Reed, who brings out practical, down-to-earth wisdom from Paul's letter as he walks alongside you on this journey. He is one who speaks from experience and is a helpful guide to show you the main sights and lessons of these important chapters. Journey toward greater joy and freedom in Christ—and lose some sinful baggage along the route!

ISBN 978-1-77484-120-4 (Pbk)
ISBN 978-1-77484-121-1 (Ebook)
104 pages; 6 x 9"
Published June 2023

An imprint of H&E Publishing
hesedandemet.com

Discover other titles from Heritage Seminary Press

Paul and His Christian Mission
By Michael Azad A.G. Haykin
Includes Study Guide

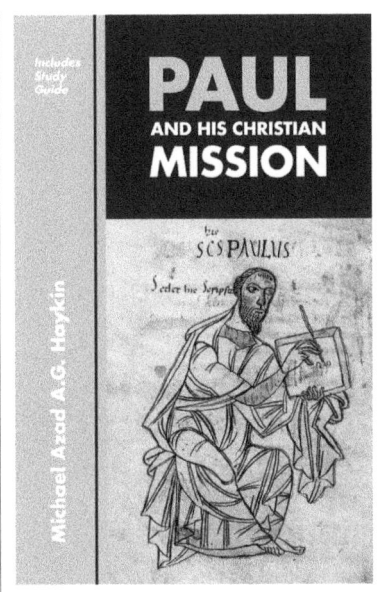

The mission of the apostle Paul is central to the New Testament, where it was vital in the establishment of the early church and spreading the gospel throughout the world of his day. This study provides a concise but rich view of Paul the man and Paul the missionary. At his conversion to Christ, Paul was given a clear mandate to bring the gospel to the Gentiles. Paul loved the church, and he was zealous to win the lost to Christ. He appreciated and cultivated co-labourers in the work of the gospel, as he depended on the power of the Holy Spirit.

Paul's experience challenges the reader. Study guide questions are provided to help reflect on and apply the things that are learned in this short, focused study of Paul's life.

ISBN 978-1-77484-106-8 (Pbk)
ISBN 978-1-77484-107-5 (Ebook)
88 pages; 5.5 x 8.5"
Published December 2022

An imprint of H&E Publishing
hesedandemet.com

Dominus Deus fortitudo mea | The sovereign LORD is my strength

www.ingramcontent.com/pod-product-compliance
Ingram Content Group UK Ltd.
Pitfield, Milton Keynes, MK11 3LW, UK
UKHW031438020125
3925UKWH00030B/271